The Home Office That Works!

Make Working at Home a Success— A Guide for Entrepreneurs and Telecommuters

2016 Edition

Updated throughout, with new sections on telecommuting, cloud computing, and co-working

Joseph W. Webb, Ph.D.
Richard M. Romano

Disclaimer: This book is based on the experiences and the research efforts of the authors. When setting up a new business, be sure to get the advice of trained professionals, such as tax advisors and others. The authors are not liable for any losses, financial or other, from following or implementing the ideas in the text.

Cover by Richard Romano.

This book was printed in the United States of America.

Strategies for Management, Inc.
3650 Rogers Road #275
Wake Forest, NC 27587
(919) 889-2760

Dr. Webb and Mr. Romano are available for one-on-one consulting, keynote speaking, workshops, Webinars, planning meetings, business discussions, organization events, and presentations about this book, or about other topics related to print, media, and marketing. Contact the authors at authors@homeofficethatworks.com for more information.

Sign up for *The Home Office That Works!* twice-monthly enewsletter at http://eepurl.com/bt00dr.

The Home Office That Works!
2016 Edition

Make Working at Home a Success—
A Guide for Entrepreneurs and Telecommuters

Find Us Online!

E-mail: authors@homeofficethatworks.com

Website: www.homeofficethatworks.com

Blog: homeofficethatworks.com/blog

Enewsletter sign-up: http://eepurl.com/btO0dr

Facebook: www.facebook.com/HomeOfficeThatWorks

Twitter: twitter.com/homeofficeworks

LinkedIn: www.linkedin.com/groups/Home-Office-that-Works-7430166

Table of Contents

Take a Deep Breath...

College students looking to earn extra cash. Moms who want or need to work but are frustrated with child care options. House-husbands who want to spend less time on the road and more time with their families. Retirees who always wanted to pursue another interest or just want to supplement their income. The downsized and laid off. Entrepreneurs who can't imagine spending their day in a cubicle. Workers fed up with the rat race. The list could go on. More and more people are choosing to work from, or run business-es out of, their homes for a whole host of reasons.

Of those individuals who work from home:

- almost one-third are 55 or older

- they are 13 percent more likely to be married

- they have 12 percent higher family income

- half have graduated college (a rate more than 50 percent higher than all workers)

- 45 percent are self-employed, 55 percent are employees

- 15 percent are in finance or real estate, 17 percent are in pro-fessions, and 24 percent are in education or social services

- more than 25 percent work more than eight hours per day

- 75 percent work thirty-five or more hours per week
- 25 percent work seven days a week
- almost one-third have irregular schedules

In 2010:

- nearly 13.5 million people worked at home
- about four million were telecommuters or other kinds of employees
- about 9.5 million were running home businesses

It's reasonable to assume that the number has only increased since then, especially with today's communications like smartphones, computer tablets, and other products.

Some more recent data from the Bureau of Labor Statistics (BLS) point out:[1]

- On the days they worked, 85 percent of employed persons did some or all of their work at their workplace and 23 percent did some or all of their work at home. Employed persons spent more time working at the workplace than at home—8.0 hours compared with 3.2 hours.

- From 2003 to 2014, the share of employed persons who did some or all of their work at home on days they worked increased from 19 percent to 23 percent. During this same period, the average time employed persons spent working at home on days they did so increased by 37 minutes (from 2.6 hours to 3.2 hours).

- Self-employed workers were nearly three times more likely than wage and salary workers to have done some work at home on days worked—58 percent compared with 20 percent. Self-employed workers also were more likely to work on weekend days than were wage and salary workers—46 percent compared with 33 percent.

[1] See http://www.bls.gov/news.release/atus.t05.htm.

This Book Is Different

It's relatively easy to find how-to books about the *types* of businesses you can run from home, and there is no shortage of blogs and websites that offer—usually in "listicle" form—tips for managing some specific aspect of working from home. But it's hard to find comprehensive information in one place about what it takes to create a working environment that is conducive to productivity and creativity without negatively impacting your personal life and the people (and pets) who share your space. It can be a delicate balance, and the purpose of this book is to help you strike it.

Earn $$$ From Home!

We want to clarify from the start that this book deals with running a legitimate home-based business. There is no lack of scams out there, all promising big bucks with a minimum investment of time and effort. Self-employment is not for the fainthearted. If you're tempted by offers of a $100,000+ income doing billing, stuffing envelopes, assembling widgets, etc., proceed at your own risk. This is such a big concern that the U.S. Small Business Administration has a section of its website about how to spot these scams.

Managing work is always easier when the work is someplace else. When work is done where you live, however, it can be a bit like worlds colliding and thus requires a different approach. The decision becomes even more complicated if you have to make it quickly or with less than exuberant enthusiasm, such as after a downsizing or if your company has abruptly turned you into a telecommuter. Regardless of how it's made, the decision to integrate your work space into your living space and your family life is best made with time, care, and a healthy dose of realism. As with most new undertakings, success generally proceeds in one-step-forward, two- (or more) steps-back fashion. This book is designed to minimize the stumbling right from the start, no matter what kind of business you choose to pursue.

Many people who start businesses from home do so because they simply can't afford outside office space or they are concerned about paying the rent if income is slow or is subject to peaks and valleys. Of course, some businesses require outside space from the outset. It's hard to run a manufacturing business in a spare bedroom.[2] But for a service, professional, or information business, that spare room just might be the perfect fit.

Don't Work in Your Pajamas

Not having to worry about investing in a business wardrobe typically ranks high on the list of advantages of working from home, but the first piece of advice we are going to give you is, don't work in your pajamas. Whenever people talk about working from home, they always seem to stress the advantage of being able to "work in your pajamas." Granted, it's really just a metaphor, but one of the ways of making working at home feel like work is to dress as if you were at work. This is not to suggest that you should wear a suit and tie in your own home office, although we do know some folks who do. But there's something to be said for pulling yourself out of bed and dressing more appropriately to approach your business day. Doing so can help you get into the psychological mindset required for the discipline of the home office. At the same time, it communicates to others in the household (and neighbors who might ring your doorbell) that you are at work and thus should not be interrupted (see Chapter 2).

A more practical reason, though, is that video calls and Skyping are becoming more and more common, and people get impressions about you from how you appear on camera. Sure, you can wear a nice shirt or blouse and still wear your crazy colored Bermuda shorts. Just don't stand up during your call.

When we find ourselves stressed, either getting to or from work or while at work, it's easy to let our imaginations take us to a place where we could work peacefully at our own pace. Our thoughts naturally turn to calm, pleasant images of contented productivity within the confines of our home. We can be near our families, the fridge, and the restroom while being away from the hassles of commuting and

[2] Despite all those computer companies like Apple that started in a garage.

office dramas. We can be masters of our own calendar. And yet these visions of paradise quickly fade when we discover what working from home *really* involves. It doesn't take much for reality to come crashing through the front door. That's because we tend to put the emphasis on the wrong word. "Working at *home*" should really be "*working* at home." They're deceptively similar phrases but differ drastically in meaning. The placement of the italics makes all the difference.

The tasks that we suddenly need to handle ourselves can be overwhelming. It may not *seem* that way at first. Answering a phone isn't a big deal—or is it? Yet, without someone to screen the call or deflect it to someone else, the one-person business owner has a decision to make every time it rings. Every phone call is a potential time sink—or a possible business opportunity. If you're a writer and you're "in the zone," that phone

This never happens.

call can derail your train of thought. Sure, it *could* be a chance for new business, but more often than not it isn't. Instead, it's probably a salesperson, or someone from the insurance company with a question, or a client who wants to make a change to something you thought was finished and delivered weeks ago. Or it's a friend or significant other who is bored at their own place of work and wants to chat. After a few calls that eat up a significant chunk of your time, you begin to wonder if administrative assistants aren't vastly underpaid.

That's just the phone. Let's not forget e-mail and Internet intrusions. And what about the doorbell—should you answer it? Is it the kid next store selling band candy? Where's that receptionist anyway? As master of your own business domain, it's incredibly easy to drown in a sea of busy work that distracts one from completing current projects or cultivating new ones.

The goal of this book is to help you set up and run a home office, whether you're running your own enterprise or you're a full- or part-time telecommuter. After all, everyone thinks that as long as they're connected to the Internet, they can work at home or anywhere they choose. Sure, you can *pretend* that you're working by answering e-mails all day or leaving your instant messaging program on, but when it comes time to get real, productive work done, you need more than an Internet connection.

This book goes step-by-step through the logistics of working at home, discusses the potential pitfalls and possible solutions, and suggests ideas for maximizing your at-home productivity—and, perhaps most importantly, your *happiness* during that productivity. After all, a happy worker is a productive worker.[3] Like any self-respecting how-to book, there are checklists, action items, and self-assessment quizzes. We will also share some of our own experiences along the way.

So let's start our journey home. Take a deep breath. It will be okay.

Know Your Strengths

Since the first edition of this book was published in 2013, we have partnered with a company called Peak Focus to offer tools for self-evaluation and professional development. Specifically, Peak Focus has an assessment called the Greatest Strengths Report that will help you identify your strengths and understand your challenges. Knowing what your greatest strengths are allows you focus on what you're good at—and communicate those strengths to prospective employers or clients and on social media like LinkedIn.

Assessments like the Greatest Strengths Report are not just for telecommuters. Even if you don't want to share the results, completing these assessments early in the process of starting your business—or just working at home—can help you prioritize what you do well, and know what to avoid so as not to undermine the process.

We will be referring to the Greatest Strengths Report occasionally in the text, but see page 208 for more information.

---

[3] Unfortunately, too few managers understand this concept, ultimately creating the kinds of toxic work environments that motivate people to want to work from home.

CHAPTER

Welcome Home!

"The most important work you and I will ever do will be within the walls of our own homes."

—Harold B. Lee, religious leader

"Home is where the heart is, so your real home's in your chest."

—Joss Whedon, movie and TV writer, producer

Answer these questions:

What is my motivation for working at home?

What are some of the challenges I will face?

How can I find help meeting these challenges?

If I share my home with family, do I have their support?

Can I dedicate the necessary time and energy to establish and maintain my own business?

What are my greatest strengths? What am I really good at?

What are my biggest challanges? What am I not very good at?

Congratulations on either beginning or continuing your home employment adventure. Whether you are self-employed at home or a part- or full-time telecommuter, this book is designed to serve as a practical guide to getting the most out of your home office. In these pages, we provide an overview of some common and not-so-common points to consider and cope with as you set up and work in your home office. These can include:

- *Financial and legal issues.* What is tax-deductible and what isn't? Can I legally operate my business in my residential area?

- *Logistical and practical issues.* What should my working hours be? How do I keep the kids under control? What if I live in an apartment? Where can I meet clients?

- *Promotional issues.* How do I get the word out about my business? How do I network?

- *Workspace issues.* What do people hear in the background when they call? Barking dogs? Screaming kids? ESPN highlights? What if the cable guy can only come when I'm scheduled for a critical conference call? How can I create a quiet place to work?

Different Work-at-Home Arrangements

Essentially, we can identify three basic work-at-home types:

- an individual running a home-based business
- a freelancer/independent contractor or professional
- a part- or full-time telecommuter

The following table summarizes the distinctions among the three categories.

Home-Based Business	Freelancer/ Independent Contractor/ Professional	Telecommuter or Teleworker
A small company that offers products or services to clients.	An individual who provides professional services to clients, ranging from consulting, to writing, to graphic design, to photography, to public relations, to marketing services, to professional public speaking, to... you name it.	An individual who is a full-time employee of a company—but doesn't own or run the company—and works from home either part time (say, two or three days a week) or full time. The company's headquarters may be local or located across the country, or even overseas.
Examples: graphic design companies, accounting firms, business consultancies, or manufacturers of specialty food items.	Examples: lawyer, accountant, consultant, designer, independent sales representative.	Examples: company PR representative, IT specialist, or salesperson.

There is some overlap between the two leftmost categories, but the primary difference is that the home-based business tends to be set up as a business entity for tax purposes, while the freelancer/ independent contractor/professional typically, but not always, is an individual who reports business income on his or her personal income tax return. (We'll look a these distinctions in more detail in Chapter 7.)

The rightmost category, telecommuter or teleworker, may differ in some significant respects from the first two, especially in terms of tax, insurance, and even some logistical respects (office hours and availability, e.g.). Often, company sales reps fall into the category of teleworker, as their job description requires them to travel and visit clients the majority of the time. Salespeople in different parts of the country from the home office (their *territories*) may report to a local or regional sales office, or may in fact consider their home (or even their car) their office. And, in fact, an off-site call center may actually be someone's home office.

Throughout this book we will address the significant differences among these categories.

Reasons to Work at Home—and to Not

Before you decide to set up and launch the home office, you should spend a substantial amount of time asking yourself *why* you want to do so. There are many good reasons to work from home, but there are just as many good reasons *not* to. If you envision that your days will be spent lying on the sofa eating chocolates, watching soap operas, and only occasionally doing a bit of work, you are destined to fail. Either financial circumstances and/or irate family members will exile you back out into the working world. Yet one of the advantages of a home office is that you can often set aside defined time to indulge in some of these leisure activities. One of the greatest reasons to work at home is to make managing other commitments and pursuits easier, all while being a more productive worker.

Have Cash on Hand

Before launching a home-based business, make sure you can feasibly afford to do so. You may need to take out a small business loan, and you may have a spouse who can help float you along, but you want to make sure that you have enough money to live on until your business becomes sustainable. It is generally advisable to have at least one year's worth of income in savings before you launch a business. This should be ready cash in an everyday savings or checking account; you do not want to dip into any retirement savings.

There are some obvious, and some not-so-obvious, advantages of a home office. On the other hand, it's not all a bed of roses, and there can be some pretty big disadvantages. The following table sums up the major issues you must carefully consider.

Advantages of Working at Home	Disadvantages of Working at Home
no need to commute, thus saving money on gas, car repairs, and ulcer medication	no real distinction between being "at work" and "at home," which can be fatiguing and lead to burnout
the ability to work in sync with your natural rhythms, thus enhancing your health and productivity	too many distractions—family, children, home maintenance issues, and other hazards of home life, decreasing productivity
escape from office dramas, meetings, and the other occupational hazards of the office environment	the lack of consistent, secure income
the flexibility to live where you want, improving quality of life	the lack of office camaraderie and collaboration
the ability to spend more time with your family, especially young children, as well as being able to travel at off-season times	the expense of setting up, equipping, and maintaining a home office
the ability to exercise, shop, and run errands during off-peak times of day, avoiding crowds and other hassles	having to do all the little administrative things you or your employer may once have paid someone to do
better health as you avoid being exposed to coworkers' illnesses	the need to do self-promotion, marketing, and networking
no need for a professional wardrobe everyday, saving on clothing and dry cleaning costs	the residual stigma of working from home ("You don't have a real job, do you?")
overall greater control over your life	overall too much responsibility in your life

Going Solo

While there are many advantages and disadvantages to starting a home business or launching a home office, there are also good and bad *reasons* for wanting to work from home. Good reasons can include wanting to spend more time with family while avoiding the hassle of office politics and other workplace issues. You may even see a greater financial opportunity in being your own boss. Bad reasons can include not really wanting to work at all or generally having unrealistic expectations of the benefits of working from home. It takes tremendous discipline to make a home office work effectively and productively.

But before you begin setting up your office/business, first ask yourself these questions:

- do I *really* want to do this?

- can I can dedicate considerable time and energy to this effort?

- will I be able to maintain this level of effort over time?

And, ultimately:

- *why* do I want to work from home?

In Our Experience: The Accidental Entrepreneur

The decision to work from home isn't always made deliberately. In 2000, Richard was working full time for a magazine publisher and was offered the opportunity to work with Dr. Joe's market research company, which began as a home-based business in 1987. Richard was suddenly working from a home office. Ever since, he has worked for one "virtual" company after another (a news and information portal for the graphic communications industry, which also has no centralized office, comprising a far-flung team of independent contractors) and as a result hasn't worked in a "real" office in more than twelve years. Richard's change of work venue wasn't necessarily by choice or design; it happened more or less accidentally. Many of the lessons we will be imparting throughout this book have come from our trial-and-error experiences—which we will highlight in these "In Our Experience" sidebars.

HELPS AND HINDRANCES

Rapidly-developing technologies, specifically mobile telephony and computing, have contributed immensely to making a home office possible. Smartphones like the iPhone can put just about all of your business connectivity literally in the palm of your hand. Use an iPad and, depending upon your business, your "office" can be wherever you are. And no one has to know!

Here are some of the technologies that *help* the home office...

- the Internet
- cellphones/smartphones
- computers
- tablet PCs
- instant messaging
- tele-/videoconferencing
- proximity to the fridge

...and some of the things that can *hinder* it:

- distrustful managers/employers who assume you are slacking off
- family/roommates
- pets
- home improvement issues
- personal calls
- visitors

The goal of this book is to highlight the helps and deal effectively with the hindrances.

Moving Forward

Let's begin in the next chapter with one of the most important mantras of real estate: location, location, location. And, as we'll see, "location" has a wide variety of meanings when it comes to configuring a home office.

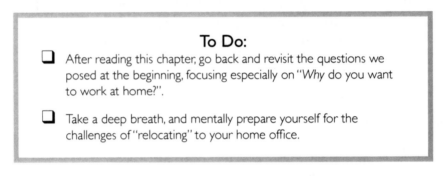

To Do:

❑ After reading this chapter, go back and revisit the questions we posed at the beginning, focusing especially on "*Why* do you want to work at home?".

❑ Take a deep breath, and mentally prepare yourself for the challenges of "relocating" to your home office.

CHAPTER

Show Them the Door

"If opportunity doesn't knock, build a door."
　　　　　　　　　　—Milton Berle, entertainer, TV pioneer

"Don't want nobody coming by without calling first."
　　　　　　　　　　—Warren Zevon, musician, songwriter

Answer these questions:

Are you legally able to run your desired business from your home?

Where in your home do you plan to set up your office?

Do you have enough privacy and quiet to concentrate on the tasks you need to perform?

Are you able to talk on the phone with clients or colleagues without background noise distracting you or the person on the other end of the line?

Do you have a place to have client meetings?

Do others in your household also work at home?

Do you need to hire employees?

Location, location, location" is a mantra that applies to running a successful home-based business, much as it does to real estate transactions. Unless you have the resources to build your own office addition, chances are you will be operating out of a makeshift office—a converted bedroom, a room in the basement, the garage, perhaps even the garden shed. You may even be running your business from a desk set up in a corner of the living room or from your dining room table. While these latter two ideas are certainly feasible, and may be necessary depending on your circumstances, you do yourself and your business a disservice by not giving your office its own space.

This chapter explains the importance of setting boundaries and avoiding distractions. There are other practical issues, too:

- zoning
- taking the home office outside or on the road
- meeting with clients/customers

Legal Matters: Zoning and Permits

First of all, before you get too far into the process of setting up your home office or business, you need to ensure that you can actually—and by "actually" we mean "legally"—run your business in your home. There was a time when zoning laws prohibited a large variety of home-based businesses, but over the years the restrictions have been relaxed. The limitations on what types of businesses you can run from home are fairly obvious and are really intended to minimize the extent to which a business is a nuisance to the neighbors.

At the same time, technology has tremendously expanded the number of opportunities that can be pursued unobtrusively in the home. If you are a freelance writer or graphic designer, sitting in your house with a computer is not bothering anyone. But if you are running a fat rendering plant in your backyard, well, that might raise a stink, in more ways than one. Gray areas include running a hair salon in your basement.

The rules regarding home-based businesses fall into three basic categories:

- *Exterior modifications and displays.* This includes restrictions on building additions onto your home, conducting business or storing items outside, erecting commercial displays, signage, and so forth.

- *Traffic.* This includes restrictions on the number of commercial visitors (customers) you can have, issues related to parking and traffic, and the number of employees you are allowed to have in your home.

- *Environment.* This includes restrictions on excessive noise, odors, flashing lights, hazardous materials storage, etc.

These are pretty obvious concerns, and they make sense from the neighbors' point of view. This is why certain parts of municipalities are zoned for commercial use while others are zoned for residential use. Zoning laws might not allow commercial vehicles, like a van or truck used in the business, to be parked in the street, or even in plain view in a driveway overnight. Bear in mind, however, that you also need to be aware of restrictions placed by homeowners or condominium associations, as they can pose dilemmas as well. Their regulations can sometimes be far more draconian than constraints imposed by local government. Before setting up your home business, be sure to consult any of these groups as well as your local planning board. It's best to invest in a little due diligence at the outset rather then become embroiled in a nasty lawsuit later. (In Chapter 7, we will discuss why you should consult a business attorney to obtain guidance on issues such as these *before* you fall afoul of the law and your neighbors.)

Zoning laws vary widely by state and municipality as well as by type of business, so we can only speak in very general terms here. The Small Business Administration (SBA) has an extensive set of online resources, including their "Home-Based Zoning Laws" (http://1.usa.gov/1xKLtec[1]). Your local Chamber of Commerce might be able to help, too.

Generally, if you're a home worker on a computer with no clients visiting you, you'll be fine. When there's a flow of traffic to your home office, however, you could have a problem. Your best start will probably be with an attorney or an accountant (both of whom may also work out of a home office).

Permits and Licenses

Just about all businesses, home-based or not, are subject to licensing and permit laws, which also vary tremendously. Permits and licenses are often required for taxation as well as data collection purposes. If you sell taxable physical products, you will need a permit to charge sales tax. If you keep an inventory of goods, your locality may charge an inventory tax. If you are running an in-home service business, such as a hair salon or a plumbing business, you will need the professional licenses required by those industries. And if your business involves federally regulated products like alcohol or firearms, you will need the appropriate legal paperwork for those items as well.

> ### States of Mind
>
> Many states have their own websites that can facilitate the process. In North Carolina, for example, BLNC.gov has online resources for prospective business owners. The National Federation of Independent Businesses (NFIB) is also ramping up their home office resources. Visit them at http://bit.ly/1GJwWFi.

If you are running an illegal business like a numbers racket or pharmaceuticals of questionable origin, sorry, we can offer you no advice, but the zoning board may be the least of your worries.

If you are a telecommuter working for a parent company located elsewhere, or are a basic information worker like a writer, de-

---

[1] Throughout this book, we have shortened long URLs to keep web addresses in the text to a reasonable length. In Chapter 10 on page 185, we have included the original long links, as well as QR codes with which you can access the links on your mobile device. We have left shorter URLs and purely tangential links in footnotes intact.

The SBA Web site has a step-by-step guide to navigating the logistics of setting up a business, customized by ZIP code and business type (inset).

signer, or public relations agent, whose main avenue of commerce is the Internet, there are fewer restrictions and less paperwork is required. Again, we can only speak in very broad general terms here, but a good place to start is the SBAs "Permit Me" online tool (http://1.usa.gov/1zKnR7n) that lets you enter your ZIP code and business type and determine what permits and licenses are required.

Once you have determined that it is legal to operate your business from your home, and you have all your paperwork in order, it's time to actually go ahead and set up the office.

Sometimes it may be possible to work at home but have the actual business at another address. There are some office buildings that rent space by the hour or the day. Seeing clients? Use that kind of facility, and you might be able to use that address as your official business address, avoiding all kinds of issues down the road. (We'll look at this option later in this chapter.)

The Perception of Doors

In the classic late 1970s/early 1980s sitcom *WKRP in Cincinnati*[2], news director Les Nessman had a desk in a large bullpen he had to share with the rest of the staff. Believing a news director—especially one who had won five Buckeye News Hawk Awards *and* the Silver Sow—should have a proper office, he put masking tape on the floor around his desk delineating where walls and a door should be.

He insisted his co-workers respect those boundaries, and he would even mime opening and closing the door.

Now, that's obviously a bit of TV comedy, but the concept of defining boundaries is critical when thinking about a home office. A door or other boundary marker is essential to getting work done.

SCOUTING LOCATIONS AND DRAWING BOUNDARIES

Think about these four home office scenarios.

- Your office is a desk in your living room, which is also the playroom for your six-year-old and his friends. You are trying to crunch numbers and field phone calls while the din goes on around you.

- Your office is essentially your dining room table, but nearly every surface in your home is not so much a piece of furniture as a filing system. Your spouse is not happy with this arrangement.

- Your office is a dedicated room in your house, but others are free to come and go as they please.

- You live in a small, one-bedroom apartment, and your office is a desk in the living room or the bedroom. You're single and have no kids, so who cares?

---

[2] See http://en.wikipedia.org/wiki/Wkrp_in_cincinnati.

How productive would you expect to be in any of these scenarios? What are some of the boundaries that can be drawn, and how can they help? Let's look at them each in turn.

Office in Shared Family Space
Having your office in a family space such as a living room, a sitting room, or even a spare bedroom that doubles as a guest room, is a recipe for non-productivity. Even assuming the kids are at school nine months out of the year, the afterschool period still needs to be managed. It's not that you want to avoid the kids entirely; one of the reasons you may want to work at home is to be able to be around your children as they grow up. But you simply can't let them have the run of your work space if you're really serious about getting a job done.

Having your office in a dedicated room—one that has a door—is a must in a situation like this. A home office must reflect a professional appearance to the outside world (i.e., your clients, employers/managers, and even neighbors). If you are making sales calls, having an important strategy or problem-solving call with a client, or participating in a teleconference with your boss, you don't want to have screaming kids, the TV, or unruly pets in the background. Not only is the noise level a distraction to you and others on the call, but it creates a negative, unprofessional impression. Your client doesn't want to, and shouldn't have to, compete against household distractions for your attention.

In some cases, though, others on the call may be colleagues with whom you are fairly close personally and thus are more accepting of the collision of the professional and the domestic. Perhaps an associate is a new parent as well, for example. Still, you do need to be careful about reinforcing all the negative stereotypes that clients and employers have about those who work at home, namely that you do not take your work seriously or that household issues will take precedence over work. Especially when dealing with new clients who are not familiar with you or the quality of your work, you need to instill in them the confidence that they have your undivided attention,

21

that they as your client are your sole concern—at least for the period of time they're talking to you.

For this reason, set time aside during the day when others know they can predictably schedule conference calls or other extended work calls with you.

The Most Important Part of the Office: The Door

The door is an important part of the office set-up, and everyone in the household needs to understand what that closed door means. A closed door means "Daddy or Mommy—or spouse, or significant other, or even roommate—is on the phone or is otherwise engaged in important work and should not be disturbed." This concept applies to couples without kids as well. Obviously if there's a medical emergency or the house is on fire, common sense has to prevail. But otherwise a closed door, perhaps with some sort of "do not disturb" sign or other indicator, such as a red cardboard circle hung from a doorknob like those seen on hotel doors (or perhaps even the "On Air" lights that TV studios use), should be treated as inviolable.

If you are forced to position your a desk in a common area of the home, you'll need to be more creative in developing boundar-

ies. Perhaps you and a neighbor could work out a kid swap, allowing both parents to enjoy some quiet time. But if not, some sort of "do not disturb" signal needs to be devised and enforced.

The Table

When working from a home office, there is a tendency for papers, magazines, office supplies, and even computers to spread throughout the home. Even when one has a dedicated room for the home office, items often "escape." The situation is a variation on Parkinson's Law:[3] your workplace will expand to fill the space

---

[3] Coined by Cyril Northcote Parkinson in 1955: "Work expands so as to fill the time available for its completion." Modern corollaries include "Storage requirements will

available for it. And few things can rile a spouse or live-in significant other like having to clear out a space on the table at dinnertime or when company is coming.

Using a kitchen or dining room table as a workspace will ultimately not succeed in the long run. It further blurs the distinction between being at work and not being at work, which can be a psychological disadvantage to working from home. A good workspace should be one that is relatively permanent. Like every other room in the house, the office should be a dedicated room or area intended for a single purpose: work. You generally don't cook in your bedroom or sleep in the bathroom. Apartment dwellers may have fewer options, but we'll deal with that issue later.

> ## In Our Experience: Birth of a Notion
>
> Dr. and Mrs. Webb ran a home office for three years prior to the birth of their son. The couple used a "tag-team" parenting approach so that each of them could get their work done. As their son got older, he was well accustomed to "the rules" about when he was allowed in the office (which was located in a finished basement) or what sort of behavior was expected when he was there. He grew up with these parameters in place. There system also led to the habit of his getting his homework done as soon as he came home from school; he worked because Mom and Dad were still working.

An Open Door Policy

Okay, so you have a dedicated office, and it even has a door. But the door is always open. Anyone is free to disrupt you at will. Depending on what you are doing, that may not be a bad thing. After all, we are not one hundred percent intent on work for the entire business day. We may just be checking e-mail, opening the physical mail, doing our social media updates, reading news and trade articles related to our business, or other low-

level tasks that may not need a great deal of attention. When doing these things, it may be perfectly fine to be interrupted. But at other

---

increase to meet storage capacity," and so forth. See http://en.wikipedia.org/wiki/Parkinson's_law.

times, we need to be intently focused on the task at hand, whether it's working on a huge spreadsheet, writing a report, or even composing an important e-mail.

In this case, setting office hours can help. Despite the fact that most people who work from home like to think they are freewheeling enough to work whenever the mood strikes, in point of fact, most of us settle into a regular daily routine. (The freedom comes in deciding what that routine is. We will look at this more closely in the Chapter 4.) Once we know what that routine is, we can assign office hours or tell friends, family, neighbors, etc., what time(s) of day are best for interruption. Appointments can be scheduled during those office hours. We also use those low-productivity times for other tasks, like running errands, going to the gym, etc.

Sometimes the work hours are dictated by others, such as family members' school hours, or the times they leave for work at a "real" job and return home. Other times, they can be scheduled around personal preference. If you're an early riser, you might find that it's preferable for you to use pre-dawn hours when the house is quiet to answer e-mails and then take a gym break at mid-morning. Night owls may get a later start and end their day at a later hour. There is no right or wrong here, just what is right or wrong for you.

The Apartment

If you're single and live alone in a studio or one-bedroom apartment, you might think it doesn't matter how you structure your work area. After all, you don't have to worry about sharing space and time with kids, a spouse, and maybe not even a pet. Who's going to complain, the houseplants? That situation may be unavoidable, and when you're young and driven, it might be tolerable. But eventually it may get tiresome, and you realize that being able to get away from work is an important aspect of mental health—especially if you have designs on not remaining a single guy or gal.

The Postman Always Rings Twice?

Some interruptions are often business-related or are otherwise unavoidable. For example, UPS or FedEx is delivering a package, the cable technician arrives to fix your Internet connection, or the mail carrier has a package you need to sign for. Maybe you have even had to call a plumber to fix a leak. If there is someone else in the house, you can instruct them to deal with it, but if you're alone, you'll obviously have no option but to deal with the visitor yourself, and nine times out of ten, it won't be an issue. Even at a full-time office job, we often have these kinds of interruptions. However, what if you are on an important conference call and UPS knocks? Or the cable company schedules you for that exact moment between nine and five—which is as specific as you can usually get with many cable companies—to come?

In some cases, a little advance planning can help. Try to make appointments for service providers on days when you don't have any important calls scheduled. As for delivery people, you usually never have any idea when you'll be getting a package. In those cases, right before getting on a call, tape a note to the front door: "Please leave any packages on front steps or come back after 2:00." If you sign the note, that can serve as the delivery signature. After the call is over, check to see if anything was delivered or if there is a "we tried to deliver" tag on the door. The worst that will happen is you may have to call and reschedule delivery. This scenario is also an example of why having packages delivered to an address other than your home may be a good idea (see Chapter 3).

In a worst-case scenario, if you really need to have the plumber over, and he arrives during an important call, you may have no choice but to put the caller(s) on hold or, if you are more of a listening participant, use the Mute button to deal with a visitor without people on the call being any the wiser.

In all of these examples, the point is, if you are serious about working at home, you need a dedicated office. Depending on your specific situation, that may not be entirely possible (*à la* a one-bedroom NYC apartment), especially when you're first starting out. We'll consider some workarounds shortly, we promise.

In Our Experience: The Apartment

Richard's first home office was a desk, a filing cabinet, and a bookshelf in his one-bedroom apartment in New York City. That was all he could afford at the time. And it worked out fine until research materials began to spread to every available surface, the dinette set became an elaborate filing system (each of the four chairs was a different subject area), and having people over involved a convoluted re-organization and post-event re-re-organization. Plus, there was the psychological fact that, even in bed at night, work and sleep still shared the same space.

WHERE TO PUT THE HOME OFFICE

In order of preference, from most to least desirable, here are some ideas and options for locating a home office.

A Dedicated Room in a Finished Basement

Ideally, it would even be the entire basement. It should *not* share a space with the children's playroom, the home gym, or the pool table, and it should have a lockable door.

- *Advantages*: It is separate from the rest of the house, so it should be quiet. Everything needed for work can be self-contained within the basement office, and stairs can be a deterrent to lugging too many things to the rest of the house. It is also aesthetically appealing when entertaining guests, as work materials are not in plain sight.

- *Disadvantages*: It's a basement, so there may be temperature issues if the basement is drafty or inadequately heated in winter. Or it may be dank or buggy. If it's located close to laundry or playroom areas, you may have noise and intrusion issues. It may also be hard to get cellphone reception in the basement. It may also be difficult to get a robust WiFi signal if the wireless network router is installed elsewhere in the house.

You could just as easily substitute "attic" for "basement," and the same considerations apply. Depending on the house, the attic may not be as creepy as the basement, and may be roomy, decluttered, and decobwebbed enough to serve as an office. You may even get better cellphone reception in an attic than a basement. However, make sure your wireless Internet signal is strong enough, if that's where you decide to set up shop.

A Den or Other "Front Room"
Locating your workspace in a separate room, like Mike Brady's den office in *The Brady Bunch*, has certain advantages over a basement office. In some newer model homes, the area that once would have automatically been designated as the dining room is now being outfitted as an office as well. Either option offers some advantages over the basement office. First of all, you don't have to walk up or down any stairs to get there. Second, you may not have to deal with temperature, humidity, and cell reception issues. Third, assuming that most basements are at least partially below ground level, a den with a window would provide natural light. Depending on the layout of the house, the den can be separated from the flow of traffic, yet be near enough so that amenities (food, coffee, rest room) are within easy reach. The downside is that it may not be separate enough and may be too close to living quarters. So you might be pressed into service to resolve a family crisis or find out who broke Mom's favorite vase.[4] Anyway, a family room, parlor, or sitting room may be easily converted into an office.

- *Advantages*: Potentially separate and quiet, yet close to rest of living quarters. Cell and wireless network reception can be better than in a basement. Availability of natural lighting.

- *Disadvantages*: May not be far enough from loud, distracting living quarters. May be aesthetically unappealing, especially if the rest of the house was decorated with a consistent look or style.

A Converted Bedroom
Depending on the size, layout, and demographics of your household, you may be able to dedicate a spare bedroom as an office. Bedrooms

[4] Yes, we are overly preoccupied with 1960s/1970s TV sitcoms.

usually have doors, and a locking doorknob can be easily installed, if there isn't one there already. This kind of arrangement is perfect in empty nests after the kids have left home. It may be less ideal at a younger age, when the prospect of having kids is on the horizon and you may need to reserve the bedroom for them. It would also be best not to have the room also serve other purposes, such as a sewing room, TV room, etc. A converted bedroom is an ideal office space in an apartment. Many work-at-home people specifically rent two- or three-bedroom apartments and designate one bedroom as the office.[5]

- *Advantages*: Like the basement office, it is relatively separate from the rest of the house, helping with quiet and self-containment. Unlike the basement office, there may not be temperature or weather issues. Cellphone reception can be better, too.

- *Disadvantages*: Again, may be too close to the rest of the house for ideal levels of quiet and lack of distraction. If the room is on the top floor of a multistory house, again make sure that your wireless network router is near enough so you can get a strong signal.

The Guest Room
Some offices double as guest rooms (or vice versa). This is an acceptable workaround if you seldom have guests, or if they only come for weekends, holidays, or your vacations—times when you are not working.

- *Advantages*: The same advantages of a converted bedroom, which is technically what it is.

- *Disadvantages*: Disruption of work environment when guests come. Reduction of usable office space for bed, bureau, and other amenities for guests.[6]

---

[5] Depending on your budget, if you live in an apartment building, you may even be able to rent an entire separate apartment, ideally next door or across the hall, that serves as the home office. Some people with deep pockets in metropolitan areas where there are few houses, like Manhattan, go this route.
[6] Sometimes the guest bed and other amenities become absorbed into the office space.

A Desk in the Living Room

Depending on your situation, this may be the only option open to you, particularly if you are just starting out in your career (young, single people rarely own houses[7]) or have just started working from home.

In fact, if you are hesitant about the idea of working at home, this may be a good way of testing the waters without committing to the expense of a dedicated office. Still, this type of home office arrangement may fall prey to distractions, particularly if you have kids at home. In this case, you may need to adopt the Les Nessman strategy and clearly mark the boundaries of the "office." Another option would be to purchase an inexpensive, free-standing privacy screen or room divider to demarcate your working area. A privacy screen can also be a good way to indicate when the work day has begun—or ended. Take it down, and the work day has started. Put it up, and the day is over (or vice versa).

A folding screen or room divider is an easy, inexpensive way to demarcate office space.

- *Advantages*: Inexpensive, and can be efficient use of space. Convenient to the rest of the house. There should be no issues with temperature, phone, Internet access.

- *Disadvantages*: May be prone to distraction from TV, other family members, etc. Lack of privacy. May be aesthetically unappealing to have an office in plain view.

A Desk in the Bedroom

This may be a better option than the living room, depending on living arrangements and work habits. If you have a significant other, but like to work late into the night, you may not be in that relationship for very long. Also, as with the other converted bedroom options, make sure you are not too far from your wireless network router.

---

[7] We tend to think of the suburbs or rural areas as sites for home offices, but many work-at-home folks prefer to live in cities (for good reason) and thus often have little choice but to rent or buy an apartment. Many people, especially retirees, often do prefer to forgo owning an actual house and rent an apartment or buy a condominium.

- *Advantages*: Private and separate from the rest of the house, especially high-traffic areas.

- *Disadvantages*: Psychological disadvantage to sleeping in the office. May inconvenience other family members.

The Kitchen/Dining Room Table

This is the least desirable option, as it intrudes upon the rest of the family and may not be especially private or quiet. You also need to disrupt your office for meals—or vice versa.

- *Advantages*: Convenient, minimal expense in setting up.

- *Disadvantages*: Prone to disruption. Office needs to be packed up and moved during meals or when there are dinner guests.

Regardless of where you have set up your home office, be sure to draw up those boundaries we mentioned. Ensure that your office set up affords you the ability to work quietly, privately, and free of distraction when you need to.

Pod People?

If you have a yard, you are not limited to the interior of the house when locating your office. A backyard shed or small cabin or a room above a garage can be converted to an office, as long as you can control temperature and get the required cell and wireless network reception. There are even "office pods" you can set up in your yard (http://bit.ly/1zKoqhB). Some look quite silly, and you may fall afoul of the neighbors or homeowners  association (or zoning laws), but some are quite elegant and stylish. Be sure you know your local laws regarding constructing office space outside the house.

Meeting Others Outside of the Office

Now that you have identified how you will situate your home office, get out if it! In other words, the same technology that lets you work at home will let you work anywhere. Of course, your first question may be, "Why would I want to?"

Home office life can be very isolating, especially if you are the only one home all day. Just getting out for errands can keep your thinking fresh and your outlook more positive. Working at home does not, and should not, mean solitary confinement.

Depending on where you live, weather can sometimes be a factor, especially in winter. So in the interest of mental health, it can be good to go out every now and then, all the while remaining productive. Even an hour or two at the gym, especially if you have a regular group of workout buddies, can do wonders for one's sanity.

There may be other, more practical reasons for getting out of the home office. Maybe there is work being done on your home that is loud or distracting. Perhaps the power and/or Internet went out.[8] Maybe another family member is hosting a birthday party or a scout meeting. And so on.

There are many options for those times when you need to get out for extended periods but still get work done.

LIBRARIES AND BOOKSTORES

The public library is a good destination if you need a nice, quiet place to work. Libraries often make WiFi available to patrons. Some bookstores offer WiFi and even have cafés. (For those addicted to book buying, it's not free of distractions, though.) Today, Barnes & Noble locations are also good places to linger and get work done.

COFFEE SHOPS/RESTAURANTS

A coffee shop can be an excellent alternative work space. Starbucks and Panera locations, as well as many independent coffee shops, often have free wireless for customers. It is usually up to the management's discretion to allow people

Smartphone apps like Wi-Fi Finder will use your phone's location to find networks in your vicinity.

---

[8] It's always good to have backup plan for this eventuality. Know where town libraries are, since they often have workspaces and free WiFi. Local colleges often make their services available to their communities, as well.

The Changing Face of Libraries

Digital technologies are transforming public libraries. They are now less about finding and reading books and more about providing Internet and electronic resources to the community, and as such libraries are becoming destinations for teleworkers. In Saratoga Springs, New York, the local Chamber of Commerce is working with the Saratoga Springs Public Library to develop initiatives to make the library more conducive to teleworking.

to linger beyond a certain length of time without buying anything, but buying at least *one* thing—a cup of coffee or tea, a bagel, etc.— would be the courteous thing to do.

If coffee is not your thing and it's lunchtime, many restaurants and bars offer free WiFi as well (not that we advocate drinking on the job).

OUT-OF-HOME MEETINGS

Although a great deal of our interaction with clients, colleagues, and employers can be accomplished online (see Chapter 5), there are times when it is more helpful, practical, or just plain desirable to meet in person. But perhaps your home office space doesn't project professionalism or is too small to accommodate others. Perhaps meeting at home would interfere with family schedules, or maybe you have antisocial or allergenic pets. The person(s) you are meeting with might not have an office of their own either. Whatever the reason, you may need to meet with others outside the home office. A good way to meet with clients or collaborators is over a meal. A favorite restaurant—whether a chain or, preferably, an independent— can be an excellent point of contact.[9] A big, comfy booth can provide

---

[9] Actually, our last three books were largely conceived and outlined at a chain restaurant in a local mall. Since some chains may have numerous locations in a relatively small geographical area, be very specific about where the meeting will take place.

enough space to break out computers and/or notepads and get work done. It is always worth checking with the host/hostess or waitstaff to see if there is any objection. During crowded times, tables may need to be turned over quickly, and the staff may discourage diners from lingering too long. It's not usually a problem, but it's always better to ask first. If you don't overstay your welcome and can also develop a positive relationship with management and/or servers, you might be able to make this spot a comfortable, reliable location for meeting with colleagues or clients.

An added bonus is that some restaurants also offer free WiFi. In our experience, Panera Bread locations are generally amenable to customers who linger for extended periods of time. For best results, though, try to avoid peak breakfast, lunch, and dinner hours—especially as they often limit patrons to thirty minutes during peak times.

Sometimes, though, you may need to have a meeting that would not be suited to a restaurant or other public location. If, for example, you had to give a presentation, or needed the meeting to be a bit more formal and professional, the local coffee shop or casual restaurant would not be appropriate. Some restaurants do have separate rooms for private parties and functions which can serve as perfectly serviceable meeting venue if the location is open at the time you need to meet.

Other available options will be a function of budget. Public libraries often have meeting rooms or classrooms and can provide A/V facilities and equipment. Depending on the community, you may need to reserve far in advance—and some (not all) require the person booking the room to be a cardholder at the library. Some branches are more flexible about this requirement than others. Churches sometimes have classroom spaces that go unused during the week and rent the rooms out for a minimum stipend as way of raising funds. Membership in the congregation is not always required. Some even have surprisingly good A/V facilities. You may have conflicts with other events, but unless you meet on Saturdays or Sundays, they're often available.

Municipalities often have community centers that are comfortable and well outfitted. Reservations are usually required and may have to be made months in advance. If you think you will need the space often, thoroughly investigate the schedule and block out a time slot. Like church facilities, community centers are generally very affordable. As an example, the Malta, New York, Community Center charges as low as $10 an hour for a meeting room.

In Our Experience: A Word to the Ys

Your local YMCA is also worth investigating. Many YMCAs have excellent meeting rooms, equipped with the latest A/V capabilities. And it may even be free. As with any meeting space, advance reservations may be required.

Chambers of Commerce typically have meeting rooms, and—by dint of being in a Chamber of Commerce office—are professional. Availability may be limited to after their normal business hours, however, and for a nominal fee. The Southern Saratoga Chamber of Commerce has a location in Clifton Park, New

Looking for Meeting Space? Talk to Toastmasters

Depending on the type of meeting you need to have, you may be able to get a good lead on meeting space options by talking to a member or officer of your local Toastmasters club. We will talk up Toastmasters more in Chapter 5, but Toastmasters International (www.toastmasters.org) is an international organization dedicated to helping its members develop and improve their public speaking skills. Toastmasters clubs meet in a wide variety of locations, from Chambers of Commerce offices, to community centers, libraries, corporate offices, and restaurants. In London, Toastmasters clubs even meet in pubs. Toastmasters officers often need to hold events in addition to club meetings, such as speech contests, officer training sessions, regional officers' meetings, and more, and likely know all the options—especially the inexpensive ones—in any given geographical area. Over the fourteen years that Richard has been a member of Toastmasters, he has had to plan numerous events—and even find regular meeting locations for the clubs of which he is a member—and thus knows every free and for-pay meeting space in a fifty-mile radius of Albany, New York. You can search for the nearest club by ZIP code on the Toastmasters International website at www.toastmasters.org. And, as we'll advise in Chapter 5, you may even want to attend a meeting!

York, and it costs only $25 to use the meeting room after hours. Some larger real estate firms or banks might also be willing to offer a similar arrangement.

If your budget is a little heftier, nearby hotels have meeting rooms you can rent, either for the whole day, several days, or even part of the day. They offer Internet access free or for a fee, and can provide A/V equipment such as projectors and whiteboards. You don't even need to be a guest in the hotel. Hampton Inn, Holiday Inn Express, and Courtyard by Marriott are some of the lower-cost options, while Marriotts, Hyatts, and Crown Plazas run on the higher end. Hotels can also offer food service ranging from bottled water, to coffee service, to full-meal catering. Independently owned and operated hotels can offer a middle-ground and are worth investigating.

If you need a *really* professional location, you can actually rent corporate meeting space from a company called Regus (www. regus.com). Regus has a wide variety of services for start-up businesses, but for our purposes here, they have facilities around the

country and rent out executive offices and meeting spaces either on a long-term basis, or in fractions of a day. They aren't everywhere, but their website lets you search by ZIP code for the location nearest to you. You can book a room for up to fifty people, and they offer boardrooms, classrooms, theaters, even a "cabaret." If you really need to convey a professional or corporate appearance, Regus is a solid option. An alternative to Regus is eOffice (www.eoffice.net.)

Co-Working: Life With Supportive Strangers in the Same Space

Since the first edition of this book, we have seen the rise of co-working spaces, which can best be thought of as "the home office away from home." Basically, they are offices that offer desks and other facilities to self-employed or telecommuting individuals. Many of these locations have some bare bones office necessities, like desks, chairs, WiFi, conference rooms, and even A/V equipment. They also solve the problem that many people have with working at home: loneliness. Many of us who work at home alone during the day love the peace and quiet of the fortress of solitude—heck, sometimes it seems like we're not lonely *enough*—but just as many feel like they are in solitary confinement, and need or want others around them, even if they have nothing to do with the business they're running.

A couple of years ago, a company called DRB Business Interiors in Saratoga Springs, New York, toyed with the idea of leasing out sections of their facility to remote workers. Called Space 2 Create, remote workers, entrepreneurs, and others could rent space at various rates, ranging from $150 to $350 a month, which gives users access to the facility a few days a month or 24/7, depending on which package they chose. The location has desks and chairs (the company sells desks and chairs, so that's a given), WiFi, a conference room, A/V gear, and individual rooms for private phone calls or meetings. It's designed to facilitate creative collaboration—or foster productive independent working.

Down the Hudson River, in Beacon, New York (Beacon is the north-ernmost Metro North stop, making it easy to get to and from New York City) is the Beahive:[10] "a new kind of collaborative space for work and community," providing wha it calls "a shared, creative work environment for entrepreneurs, the creative class, microbusinesses and consultants." In 2012, they opened a third "hive" in Albany. (The second hive was in Kingston,but has since been closed. Colony collapse disorder, perhaps?) The hives include WiFi, networked printers and other peripherals, kitchen facilities, and other amenities.

You know a phenomenon is growing when it spawns its own association. Indeed, the new Global Workspace Association (GWA)[11] consists of business center and virtual office owners, co-working spaces, hotels that provide serviced workspaces, business incubators, mobile workforce service providers, managers and support staff as well as vendors who provide "workspace-as-a-service." A GWS study found that 2,100 co-working spaces existed in the U.S. as of October 2014, up 111 percent from 2013. And *Deskmag*, a co-working industry magazine, said that 90 percent of U.S. co-working spaces expected to increase membership in 2015, while 25 percent of them expected to see *significant* growth.[12] Experts point out that these types of spaces are targeted to, and are more appealing to, millennials, claiming it as part of the so-called "sharing economy."[13]

These types of facilities can be pricey—but they aren't always—and may be impractical as a permanent, full-time office space, but can serve in a pinch if you do need an outside location either to collaborate, have meetings, or just to be around other people. They can also be good for larger events. It's hard to have an office party (although it can be done) when you work from

[10] Visit http://beahivebzzz.com.
[11] Visit them at www.globalworkspace.org.
[12] Kieran Mcquilkin, "Entrepreneurs and small business owners gravitate to co-working spaces," *Richmond Times-Dispatch*, July 26, 2015, http://bit.ly/1Ip77op.
[13] Prominent examples include Uber, Lyft, and Airbnb, although we find it difficult to see how a service that charges money can be considered part of a "sharing" economy.

home, but if you need the ability to have client/colleague get-to-gethers, these types of facilities can provide a good alternative to having people in your house.

Working With Significant Others in the Same Space

In many—or perhaps even most cases—we will be working in our home offices, and at home in general, by ourselves. As we have mentioned, there may be others physically at home, but not working at home. However, there are two cases we do need to consider: when a spouse or significant other also works at home, and when you need to hire additional staff for your own home-based business.

Til Death Do You Part? When a Spouse Works at Home

What if your spouse/significant other also has a business at home, or works in your business?

Sometimes one household member has an office at home, and other finds him- or herself needing to do the same thing. This can certainly upset the applecart! We mentioned earlier that you tend to find a new rhythm to worklife when you're no longer in an outside office. That rhythm is built on finding the best productive times of the day for yourself and managing the daily home patterns of others. When a member of the household  also finds themselves in a similar situation, those best productive times of the day are the ones that are in the most jeopardy. The one advantage is that in the times when other family members return to the house after school or their outside obligations, you can engage in tag-team time management. That is, one can take turns with the other home worker in defending the private work time of the other.

The Webbs have worked together almost since the beginning of Dr. Joe's business. Aside from the usual jokes about "we can't work together because we'll end up killing each other" before they started, they found great convenience in taking turns with errands and each having "alone time" with their son when he came home from grammar school. One of the challenges was in summers, when their son was home. He, too, had work assignments, where no electronic entertainment was allowed, but he had to read or keep fresh with math or science workbooks for one hour a day when he was young, and later two hours as he got older. This allowed the Webbs to have work time together for the tasks that needed their mutual attention. They also traded off evening time for quiet work in the summers for a couple of days a week.

There are times when two members of a household are in separate and distinct businesses, having no shared business tasks. This is somewhat different. Managing time to be with other household members is still needed, and creating a schedule for that is important. When working in the same business, the tasks of the day can determine the availability that each of you have. When working in different businesses, it's not always possible to be so flexible.

It's very helpful to keep three calendars, and it's not as hard as it sounds. We suggest keeping online calendars for each other, using a resource such as Google Calendar, where each person can see the time obligations of the other. There should also be a family calendar where school events, doctor appointments, sports commitments, home repair appointments, vacations, birthdays and other social events can be kept. (The smartphone app Evernote is quite useful for these purposes; see https://evernote.com.)

It's also helpful to keep a whiteboard in a place where it can be easily seen. Each person should take one side of the board (left and right or top and bottom) and post key appointments, especially mutual ones, as a reminder, or to leave messages for each other as needed.

Two home offices is not a big challenge, though it may seem that way at first. Feeling your way through the first few weeks will have its ups and downs and issues. Everyone develops schedules and rules that make it work. We have known many couples who work at home in separate businesses and have been very pleased with the results financially and in their relationships.

Be sure you have non-work time, both together and alone. Whether you are in the same business or not, work can consume you and dominate your time together. It's helpful to set a rule that business discussions won't be had at certain times of the day unless absolutely necessary. There's a time and place for everything, and getting away from business, just like coming home from work at the end of the day, is important.

Intruder Alert! Bringing in Additional Staff

As your business grows, you may find that you need additional help. You may need someone to take over administrative and other "grunt work"—getting the mail, text or data entry, and so on—but may also need  extra staff to handle higher-end functions of your business, such as a second graphic designer, a research assistant, a copywriter, and so on. It is also not uncommon these days to bring in additional staff or interns to do social media updates.

One way of handling this is to simply have the additional staff person working out of *their* own home, and schedule in-person meetings once a day, once a week, or as needed. As long as the additional person has his or her own computer and whatever other resources may be needed (appropriate software, e.g.), they can work wherever they like. And if you have fears that they will "slack off" if they work at home, just remember that you are in the same boat! (Also feel free to give them a copy of this book.)

Sometimes, though, you need to bring the person in-house—and by in-house we mean "in *your* house." Much of this topic is beyond the scope of this book, but we'll offer a little bit of guidance if your circumstances require additional staff.

Good Help is Hard to Find

If you need help, where do you find it? First, start with family and friends. Is there a niece or nephew, or an in-law, or a friend that could use a few extra bucks? If they fit the skill set that is required for what you need them to do, that can be an option. But be careful. If the working relationship doesn't work out it may damage a personal relationship. So while one's own social circle can be a good employment pool, it may be best to hire a stranger.

A good alternative would be the Career Services office of a nearby college or university, which often posts jobs open to students. Just be sure you are *very* specific about the type of experience you need. If you require that an employee know a certain piece of software—Photoshop, Excel, etc.—be sure you spell that out. Also find out what the going rate for what you require is (Career Services can help with that) and don't be shy about offering a buck or two above that. Very often you get what you pay for.

Hive Minds

One of the benefits of co-working spaces (see page 36) is that you may find the resources you need there. This is also a good reason to be active in your Chamber of Commerce or other groups. When you work alone, you actually need to be networking more, and this is one of the reasons.

Speaking of students, if you need access to expensive online data sources and other materials, a student can be an excellent resource for doing research. Academic libraries often carry materials unavailable at a public library (business and other databases), and while they are sometimes available to the public, non-students/faculty frequently lack access. Either way, you can meet your student researcher at the library, plan out the project, and let them do all of the grunt work for you. Look for students who require little direction and are self-motivated.

Temp agencies can be an effective source for more or less clerical employees—transcription, word processing, etc.—but be sure that candidates meet the skills specifications you lay out beforehand. It's better to not have someone than to have someone who is constantly asking questions they should know already ("what happens when I press CAPS LOCK?"). Temp agencies do not necessarily like sending people to home offices, however, and it not difficult to understand why.

One of our female colleagues has a home office and while she was married with a schoolage child, she worked home alone during the day, and when she was looking for an in-home-office part-time employee, was leery of hiring a male.

Regardless of whom you hire, there has to be a very high level of trust on both sides of the relationship.

Don't Make Them Feel at Home

We stress throughout this book that your home office should above all feel like an office, not a home. This is even more true when you bring outsiders into the office. You want to ensure that the new recruit feels like an employee, not a houseguest. Just as it is important for you to get into the psychological mindset that this is a home *office* (not a *home* office), it's even more important for your employee(s) to be in the same mindset.

You will need to give some thought to where an additional employee will physically work. If your office is in your bedroom, well, that could get very awkward very fast. On the other hand, if you have a big, spacious basement office—maybe with room dividers or even separate rooms—that would be far more practical. Sometimes you may need to have private, sensitive, or confidential calls, so you want to make sure you can have some privacy from your employee should you need it.

If you have in-home-office help, they may require their own computer and other amenities (phone, desk, office supplies). It's tempting to just have them bring in their own laptop computer—assuming they have one—but if they are going to be working with sensitive files, you may not want those files to leave the office.

Other considerations when taking on employees can include:

- Can they use their own cellphone as their work phone? Would they want you to pay some portion of the bill? How much?
- Do you have a separate bathroom?
- Do you have a separate business entrance?
- Will the employee need to come in when you are not around? Will you want to entrust this person with keys to your home?
- Will parking be an issue?

If you hire someone to work in your house, they may need to be a W-2 vs. 1099 employee (see Chapter 7). If their work reaches a particular hourly threshold, you may be required to offer them medical and Workmen's Compensation insurance. Be sure to check the requirements in your particular state and/or municipality.

Then again, if your business is successful enough that you do need to take on additional help, you may be in a position to build onto your existing home—or even custom-build a new home—with a home office in mind.

There are many other considerations—legal, personal, and practical—when taking on employees, and if you find yourself in this position, there are many other books and resources available should you require more information than this brief overview has provided.

Moving Forward

Once you have identified the optimal location for your home office, defined its barriers, and come up with effective "do not disturb" indicators, it's time to start dealing with some of the logistics of setting up the office. This includes furnishing it, but also setting up telephone service, Internet access, and mail delivery. And if you're thinking, "Can't I just use my home phone/Internet/mail?" the answer is "yes"—but you may not want to. We'll explore that decision in the next chapter.

To Do:

❑ Check the Small Business Administration website (http://1.usa.gov/1xKLtec) and review the summary of zoning laws and see if any of the issues raised affect your home business.

❑ Consult the by-laws of any homeowners, condo associations, co-op boards, etc., you may be a member of to ensure that you are not risking violation by setting up your home business.

❑ Review the Small Business Administration's section on permits and licenses and make sure you get the correct paperwork. It may also be in your best interest to consult a small business attorney to ensure that you are doing everything correctly.

❑ Identify the optimal location in your home for your office. Be sure to clearly define the boundaries of the office space. Develop a system for communicating "do not disturb" messages.

❑ If you think you will need to take client or colleague meetings outside your home, start to draw up a list of potential locations. Remember that some places like community centers require reservations far in advance, so get a sense of the availability and expense if your options in case you need to plan a meeting without much advance notice.

CHAPTER

A Place for Your Stuff

"A house is just a place to keep your stuff while you go out and get more stuff."
—George Carlin, comedian

"There is no reason for any individual to have a computer in his home."
—Ken Olsen, co-founder of Digital Equipment Corp.

Answer These Questions:

What is your business phone number? Is it the same as your home phone number? What happens when another household member is on the phone when you need to keep the line open for client calls?

Do you have a separate business computer? Or will you use the general household computer?

Do you have high-speed Internet access?

Are you familiar with cloud computing?

How reliable is the cellphone signal in your office location?

How will you handle business mail as well as incoming and outgoing packages?

Now that you've staked out your home office space, what should you put in it? More to the point, how do you handle the logistics of actually running the business? What should you do about phone and Internet service? What's the best way to handle mail and deliveries? What are the advantages and disadvantages of sharing services with the rest of your household?

This chapter will look at outfitting your office space. This will include not just furniture but options and ideas for Internet connectivity, phone service, and even handling physical mail delivery.

Furnishing the Office

Some of these items on the following list might seem obvious, but often it's the most glaringly obvious items that are overlooked. Here are some fundamentals:

FURNITURE AND ACCESSORIES

- desk
- chair
- chair mat
- desk lamp
- floor or ceiling lamp
- waste basket
- paper shredder
- filing cabinet
- shelving, for books, software, and/or work-in-progress
- telephone
- copier/scanner/fax machine or multifunction device

Three Chairs for Furniture!

When setting up a home office, don't skimp on office furniture. Specifically, invest in a good desk. Try to avoid that unassembled particle-board furniture you can get on the cheap in office superstores. There was a time when it was of decent quality, but over the past decade it has declined significantly. It also does not lend itself to disassembly and reassembly if, for example, you move. (Moving companies also make customers sign waivers absolving them of responsibility for damage to particle-board furniture.) The same goes for bookshelves. Cheap shelves can develop a pronounced sag, often in a very short period of time, and eventually just collapse. As for chairs, office superstores offer many options in a wide price range, but be sure to try them out first. You're going to be spending a lot of time in that chair, so make sure that it is both ergonomic and comfortable.

Don't overlook used desks and shelving found at estate sales, going-out-of-business and liquidation sales, and even on Craigslist. Used furniture dealers are also worth checking out. Depending on your budget, you can also buy high-quality modular furniture online or offline.

Many furniture stores now have sections for home offices since working at home has become more common. Many furniture stores also now have home office departments, so don't just look at what the office superstores have to offer. Taft Furniture (www.taftfurniture.com) and Winners Only (www.winnersonly.com) are two stores with which we have had good experiences.

COMPUTER HARDWARE

Computer

It's crucial that you get a separate computer for your business, especially if your home computer is shared with other members of the family. You don't want to fight with others for accessibility, or risk a family member (and not just a child) damaging the computer, or accidentally deleting something they shouldn't. Also, do you want family members playing around with your business tax records on the computer? There are ways around this (having separate password-protected user accounts on the same computer), but having a separate computer would be best. A laptop would be the preferable to a desktop tower (and tower PCs are becoming almost as quaint as those old room-sized mainframes from the 1960s and 70s), as the laptop gives you portability if you need to work remotely. It may even be possible to skip a computer entirely and rely on a tablet (see "iPhones, Tablets, and Apps" below).

Wireless Router
See "Taking Your Business Online" below.

Printer
If you need copying, faxing, scanning,[1] and printing capabilities, you can purchase all-in-one "multifunction" devices at Staples, Walmart, or online.

External Computer Storage
An external hard drive is a great place to back up files, and the cost of computer storage is always dropping.[2] Prior to the 2013 edition of this book, a three-terabyte (3TB) external hard drive could be had for $120; just before to the 2015 edition, a 2TB drive was a mere $75. Cloud storage may also be a good substitute. (See "Cloudland" below.)

The computer storage situation has developed a new wrinkle. Aside from using cloud software, there are now more "personal cloud" products available, often sold to consumers for storing entertainment media. Seagate has its "Personal Cloud" and Western Digital has "MyCloud."[3] You can now work productively more than ever with a tablet or Chromebook rather than a desktop or laptop,

---

[1] Actually, a smartphone camera can serve as a decent ersatz scanner. Depending on your specific needs (i.e., scanning receipts) you may not need anything more elaborate. You can even download an optical character recognition (OCR) smartphone app that will convert a photographed document to editable text that can be transferred to a computer and further edited and cleaned up. Richard has done this and it works better than you'd think it would.

[2] It is imperative that all your important files are backed up regularly so that you can restore your work in the event of a computer or human error. The hard drive is usually the first part of any computer to die. Richard once accidentally spilled an entire mug of coffee into his laptop computer causing it to explode. Neither situation is desirable.

[3] Read reviews at http://bit.ly/1MhQoVZ.

and you never have to sync files because the files are not resident on an individual computing device.

Webcam

Webcams are often built in to most recent laptop models, but if not you may need to pick one up (<$100) if you plan to participate in videoconferencing or Skype. Also, the last few versions of the iPhone, iPad, and other smartphones/tablets have built-in video-cameras that will let you videoconference.

Whatever Hardware You May Require for Your Specific Business

A high-end scanner? A professional quality digital camera? High-end video and/or audio capabilities?

Don't Forget Tech Support

What happens when your computer stops working? Or your e-mailbox has crashed and you can't access your saved messages? Or any of the hundreds or thousands of things that can go wrong with a computer? If you are technically proficient, you may just be able to do your own troubleshooting and repairs. Even better, you may have someone else in your household who is highly technological—a teenager, for example. Friends and neighbors might also be able to offer tech support.

Failing these options, you may have to search out local computer repair shops. If you use a Mac, there may be an Apple Store nearby, and its Genius Bar can often help with troubleshooting. If you are a Windows user, Best Buy's Geek Squad or local independent computer repair shop could probably help.

It's a good idea to identify a competent source of technical support *before* you have an issue. After all, if you have computer problems, you may lose Internet access, which limits your ability to get help. (For example, a modem manufacturer in the 1990s once did literally put in their user manual, "If you have problems, visit our online technical support site." Of course, if you have problems with a modem, you can't actually go to an online site, but you might have to run to a friend's house or to the town library.) Ask your Facebook or LinkedIn friends if they have any recommendations. Finding a reliable, economical computer repair person is like finding a reliable, economical auto mechanic. As is the case with many services, word-of-mouth recommendations are often the best.

COMPUTER SOFTWARE

A lot of the basic software that you will need will be pre-installed on your computer—e-mail program, Web browser, instant messaging, etc. Some other items you may want to consider:

Word Processing Software

Microsoft Word, for example. You may find it preferable to invest in the entire Microsoft Office suite that includes Word, PowerPoint (for doing presentations), Excel (spreadsheet), and Outlook (e-mail). Alternatively, you can use LibreOffice, which comprises open source[4] word processing, spreadsheet, and presentation software. WPS Office was formerly Kingsoft Office and although it changed its licensing policy, as of January 2016 the company offers a free version for one computer. One caution is that free office suites don't have many templates available, especially for presentations (although WPS has many).

We have also experimented with Softmaker's office suite, which we recommend unless you are doing large amounts of statistical work. Excel offers superior chart capabilities. If you are on a Mac, Apple has Pages, Numbers, and Keynote, its own version of an office application suite. Most of these formats are roughly interchangeable with each other, although some features like formatting, images, and other items may not convert reliably. It is best to check with those with whom you will be collaborating to determine what would be the best tools to have.

Quicken/QuickBooks

These programs are popular accounting software. Depending on your proficiency, Excel or another spreadsheet program may work perfectly well. There is also a cloud version. (See Chapter 7.)

Adobe Acrobat

Acrobat is a utility for reading and/or annotating PDF (Portable Document Format) files.

---

[4] "Open source" software is free to users and has an excellent track record of reliability. Rather than being maintained by one company (like Microsoft), open source software is maintained by many contributors, often worldwide. Examples are the office suite LibreOffice, the web browser Firefox, and web page creation software WordPress.

Skype

Skype is a videoconferencing and texting application—and it's free (See Chapter 4.)

Other Software Required for Your Business

Photoshop? Graphic design and layout like Adobe InDesign? Web design? Video editing like Final Cut Pro? Audio editing like Pro Tools?[5]

CLOUDLAND

In the short time since the 2015 edition of this book, there have been significant changes in "the cloud." "Storing files in the cloud" simply means that rather than having your files stored on your own computer or on a separate disk or drive that connects to your computer, everything is stored on the Internet. Today, cloud use for computing itself, beyond just storage, is increasing significantly.

If you check your e-mail from your phone, get directions using a GPS device, or listen to music on Pandora or another music service, you've been using cloud computing. Because high-speed Internet connections have become more available and it's more common to alternate among tablets, smartphones,

> ### Software Gets SaaSy
>
> Most software is migrating to the cloud. Adobe has announced that it will no longer offer "local" versions of its Creative Suite (Photoshop, Illustrator, InDesign, etc.)—it is now the Creative Cloud. Other software is becoming cloud-based, as well, and it's safe to say that within a few years "desktop" software will be as obsolete as software distributed on floppy disk. The downside (we find) of much cloud-based software is that it is subscription-based. This is often referred to as "software as a service (SaaS)" Instead of buying the software for a one-time fee, you pay a monthly subscription charge. The upside is you don't ever have to worry about upgrading it. It is also available across all your devices.

---

[5] Before you buy computer hardware, be sure that the software you will need for your business will run on the hardware you intend to purchase. It had long been the case that a lot of software was unavailable on the Macintosh platform. That isn't always so today, but it may be. Although there is a way to run Windows and Windows applications on a Mac, it may not perform as well as it would if running on a native Windows machine, which can impact your productivity.

and desktop computers, moving files back and forth became a problem. If the files are stored in the cloud, there's a benefit to using the same software on all of those devices, but that's not always possible because of the amount of on-device storage needed for word processing and other software. So rather than install software on your tablet or smartphone, fast Internet connections can access software running on computer servers in the cloud as if they were your computer. With good connection speeds, it's hard to tell the difference. Most cloud-based software works within your everyday Internet browser, although sometimes you might need to download a special phone or tablet app that is specially designed to interface with the cloud software.

More and more software companies are creating cloud versions of their software; Microsoft Office 365 (products.office.com) is a cloud version of the Office suite, while Adobe's Creative Cloud (www.adobe.com/creativecloud.html) takes Photoshop, InDesign, Illustrator, and the company's other high-end design tools into the cloud. Intuit now offers QuickBooks cloud accounting (quickbooks. intuit.com/cloud-accounting-software), and FreshBooks and Xero are becoming popular alternatives to Quicken Cloud. To use these services, you pay a regular subscription (monthly or yearly) and you get desktop versions of the software (so you can work offline) as well as some quantity of online storage. The desktop applications and corresponding mobile apps can access these files wherever you happen to be. This is also great for collaborating, since you can share files, as well.

Cloud-based software is not favored by everyone, and even we are a little leery of subscribing to software rather than just buying it outright, or using open source software. But however you may feel about what is known as "software as a service (SaaS)," the cloud still can offer tremendous benefits just in terms of storage. Cloud storage lets you keep all your files on a third-party system, which is a great boon as the number of devices we may be using increases.

What's In a (File) Name?

As you start working on projects and accumulating project files on your computer, you will at some point realize that finding specific files can become an elaborate scavenger hunt. The search becomes more complicated when you need to locate a client project folder, a Word file, or an Excel spreadsheet from two or more years ago.

When you are just starting out, it is best to adopt a set of file naming conventions so that you can easily find things at a later date. Never assume you will remember! Your naming system doesn't have to be overly elaborate or convoluted,but it should allow you to readily find what you're looking for when you do a general file search. Windows—and, for some reason, the Mac later on—has a default "Documents" folder. Avoid it. There is no reason why all your active project folders can't simply be right at the top level on your hard drive.

You should have a separate folder (or directory) for each client, and within each folder, a separate folder for each project. Files within those project folders should clearly and succinctly indicate what the contents of the file are. If you and others send revisions back and forth, be sure to include the date (or even the time) of the revision in the file name, as well as the initials of the person who made the last revision. (It's not always a good idea to rely on the save date/time stamp the software automatically adds.) For example, "Project X-rr-040113-113pm." That indicates the name of the project ("Project X"), the initials of the person who revised it ("rr"), and the date ("04-01-13") and time ("1:13 pm") that revision was made or received. Your clients or colleagues may not have the same naming conventions as you; when you receive files from them, always save them in the appropriate folder using your own naming conventions so you can identify the correct document to work on. This may all sound needlessly anal retentive, but it can save a lot of time and effort in the future.

This way, you can always find what the latest version of a file is, and not accidentally send someone an early draft. Adding the word "FINAL" to the file name of the final version isn't always a help, either, as there are inevitably changes beyond that, and it is not uncommon to have seven different files all called "FINAL."

There is a growing number of cloud storage services. A few to investigate are:

- Amazon Cloud Drive (www.amazon.com/clouddrive)
- Box.com (www.box.com)

- Copy.com (www.copy.com)

- Dropbox (www.dropbox.com)

- Microsoft OneDrive (onedrive.live.com)

- Western Digital Personal Cloud (www.wdc.com)[6]

- CloudUp (cloudup.com)

They all have a selection of plans, from very basic free plans that offer relatively low storage capacity (usually around 10 or 15 gigabytes), only one user, and limits on individual file size, to mid-range plans for $10–$20 per month that offer more storage and the ability to add users, to high-end enterprise plans for larger businesses. They also offer the ability to access stored files on a variety of desktop, laptop, and mobile devices. Amazon's Cloud Drive is free to Amazon Prime members, as well as owners of Kindles, Fires, or other Amazon mobile devices.

Although we have not tried all of these services, Richard uses Dropbox—the basic free edition—to share large files (like book production files) with colleagues. Dr. Joe dislikes Dropbox and vastly prefers Box.com. Joe also uses copy.com, but thinks Box is better, especially for business. We've found OneDrive to be very slow (so is Dropbox for things like video). CloudUp is very generous with free space (200GB!).

Most people also don't realize that when they get a free Gmail account they also get free use of Google Documents *and* have free cloud storage using Google Drive. Very few people take advantage of their Google Drive accounts—and they should. It is an excellent way of sharing files without having to email them back and forth, or even monkey around with Dropbox, et al.

All of these services boast high security, but for those of us who are paranoid about hacks or outages—as well as the fact that we are not always connected to the Internet—it is always a good idea to have copies stored locally and/or on an external hard drive.

[6] Western Digital Personal Cloud is a device and not really a service.

It could be argued that the combination of cloud computing and cloud storage is eliminating the need to even have a computer, and just use a tablet or Google Chromebook.

For the common software programs you might use, such as word processing or spreadsheets, there are great benefits to cloud computing. First, you can pay a small monthly fee for the software rather than making a big purchase of software that might be as much as the computer you are buying. Second, the cloud-based software is always up to date. You don't have to worry about making upgrades or installing program fixes.

If you are concerned about not always having an Internet connection, you should be. For this reason, Microsoft's Office 365 does allow downloading of full versions of software as part of the subscription, to as many as five devices. This is one reason why we would favor using the Microsoft service rather than something like Google documents. The OneDrive service allows you to share documents with others without having to attach them to e-mails. The Microsoft service requires you to open a Microsoft e-mail account based on their Outlook e-mail product.

We've never liked Outlook on our computers as hackers always seemed to be targeting it and if you have a computer crash, you might lose years worth of e-mail. But now, Outlook is a cloud-based product, much like Gmail is, which is a big improvement. While we're not fans of Outlook and don't use it as our regular e-mail application, it does provide a convenient way of keeping your business computing life separate from your personal computing life.

If you use cloud services, you will always have free open source software to use as a backup should you not have a connection.

IPHONES, TABLETS AND APPS

We'll talk about cellphones and smartphones below, but we also want to mention tablet computers like iPads here. You may find an iPad, Samsung Galaxy Tab, Google Chromebook, or other such device essential for business. As we said earlier, not only can they more and more take the place of a "real" computer, they are far more mobile, take up less room, and arguably do more things than even desktop computers can do.[7]

Regardless of what your business is, there is probably an iPad and/or corresponding iPhone app. As a result, it is beyond the scope of this book to detail all of them.

It has even been argued that the proliferation of apps are killing the web as we currently know it, and it's not difficult to envision a day when most of what we will need to accomplish online can be done via apps rather than a web browser.

Keeping In Touch: The Connection Trinity

There are three basic elements every business needs to function:

- a mailing address

- a phone number

- an e-mail address

One could make an argument for a website, a Facebook page, or a LinkedIn page, but for the basics of conducting business, these are the Big Three. Let's look at these considerations one by one.

PLEASE, WAIT A MINUTE, MR. POSTMAN: THE MAIL

The U.S. Mail is a service we all take for granted, even if we do receive less physical mail than in the past. But when setting up a home business/office, considering how mail should be handled is an issue that requires more than just a passing thought. Specifically:

- Do you *really* want your business address to be your home address?

- Do you *really* want to receive your business mail at home?

There are a few reasons why you may answer "no" to one or both of those questions.

---

[7] See, for example, Christopher Mims. "You Can Ditch Your PC Now," *Wall Street Journal,*, November 9, 2014, http://on.wsj.com/1OKT5yG.

Why would you *not* want your business address to be your home address? One reason would be that you run the risk of having people drop by unannounced. If you publish your business address on your Web site or in other promotional materials, clients and salespeople would rightly conclude that it was, well, a business address. Therefore, there would be nothing wrong with stopping by, which may be one of the distractions you were trying to avoid by setting up a home office in the first place.

Another reason involves the second question: where do you receive your mail? There are certainly advantages to simply receiving all your business mail at your home address. It's convenient, and it's free. You don't have to pay for a mailbox anywhere, and you don't have to leave your premises to get your mail, the latter an important consideration when there is bad weather.

One disadvantage to receiving business mail at home is that if you live alone and travel with any frequency, or you and the whole family go away on vacation for any length of time, you run the risk of mail piling up. You can have the Post Office hold your mail—but you can't have UPS, FedEx, and other private carriers hold any packages. And these carriers usually have pretty lax policies regarding residential neighborhoods. Unless instructed otherwise, typically by the shipper, they will just leave packages on the front steps of the house. As a result, they can be stolen or, even worse, give the impression that no one is home, inviting burglary. Packages left outside can also be subject to rain and snow, potentially damaging the contents. You can leave notes on the door telling potential deliverers that you are

> ## Weather or Not to Receive Packages at Home...
>
> In residential areas, it's common for delivery services to leave packages outside houses and apartments if no one is home—exposed to cold, rain, snow, and potential theft. If you plan to be receiving items that that may be damaged by exposure to the elements, even if in a box (Richard used to review scanners and digital cameras, for example), consider a UPS Store mailbox.

57

away. But those notes may be overlooked or ignored; they may also advertise that no one is at home.

As with anything else, you have choices in where to have your mail delivered.

Post Office Box

The P.O. box is a relatively inexpensive option. The box is located in the lobby of your local post office, and you don't have to worry about mail piling up someplace, exposed to the elements if you are away for an extended period of time.

- *Advantages*: Convenient for receiving mail, not outrageously expensive. There are different mailbox sizes to choose from, based on how much mail you get—or think you're going to get.

- *Disadvantages*: The Post Office cannot accept UPS, FedEx, or other private carriers' deliveries, which may defeat the purpose of getting an out-of-home mailing address. You are also limited to getting mail during the Post Office's business hours.

The UPS Store

Formerly called Mailboxes Etc., The UPS Store is a mailing and office services franchise, usually located in strip malls. Although owned by UPS, they are run by individual franchisees.

- *Advantages:* They can receive any shipper's deliveries, and they can ship packages out by services other than UPS. They do add a service charge for non-UPS packages. They tend to have longer hours than the Post Office, and during the Christmas shopping and shipping season are even open on Sundays. You can also have access to mail when they are closed, if you have a special key or code to let you in.

- *Disadvantages:* If you receive a really large, heavy package, you have to get it home somehow. This is not a problem if you are relatively athletic, but it can be if you have a small car. Also, when you sign up for a mailbox, you sign a waiver that absolves the franchisee of any blame for missing or damaged mail. If there is a change of store ownership and the location is abruptly closed for a long period of time—and you cannot get your mail—the Post Office does not go out of its way to help you.

A potential concern—with *both* these options, it turns out—is hoping that either the UPS Store retail location or the Post Office branch stays where it is for the length of time you plan to run your business. Franchises go in and out of business all the time, and the Post Office is closing locations around the country. There is no easy way of predicting the longevity of your mail delivery site, but fortunately, change of address and mail forwarding forms are easy and convenient to distribute.

HANGING ON THE LINE: THE PHONE

A telephone is a must for any business, of course, and although more and more business communication takes place using some sort of Internet application (e-mail, instant messaging, Skype, FaceTime), the telephone is still necessary to be able to communicate with people who may either dislike or not be especially proficient with electronic media.[8]

You have several choices when it comes to telephony.

Landline

The old standby. The phone connects to physical wires. Landlines are generally reliable, even if today's handsets don't come anywhere close to matching the superb sound quality of the old Bakelite phones of yesteryear.

- *Advantages:* Decent call quality and reliability, and cordless handsets give you the ability to move around the house or even

---

[8] Cable providers like Time-Warner, and now their satellite-based counterparts, offer comprehensive bundles of services that include cable TV, Internet, and telephone. Some people like the convenience, and it can be an economical option. However, others dislike relying on a single provider for every service, especially if the cable often goes out in a storm (or for no discernible reason whatever) leaving you without all services simultaneously.

the yard. You can (and should) get a separate landline just for your business so you don't have other family members intercepting business calls or tying up the line. It is also a good way to manage distractions as you only give your business number to clients, colleagues, or employers, caller ID notwithstanding.

- *Disadvantages:* Additional expense if you also have a mobile phone and/or a home landline. You bear the responsibility for repairing any home telephone wiring problems. If you do decide to ditch the landline in favor of a cellphone at some point down the road, you'll have to notify anyone who has your old number, plus you may have to reprint business cards, stationery, etc. However, in many places, you may be able to transfer your landline number to a cellphone.

Cellphone

More and more individuals and businesses are forgoing landlines and relying solely on cellphones, specifically smartphones like iPhones or Google Android phones. If you are a telecommuter who works for a parent company, you may be issued a BlackBerry smartphone, as

Wikimedia Commons

the BlackBerry long ago found favor among corporate IT departments.[9] Before canceling landline service, though, make sure you get strong, reliable cell reception in or around your home office. Service is getting better and better, and there has been noticeable improvement in just the last five years. But still.

As stated earlier in this chapter, everything you do should project a professional appearance to clients and colleagues, and although everyone understands the limitations of cellphones, you make a poor impression if your calls drop repeatedly. It also negatively impacts

[9] By mid-2013, the BlackBerry had lost market share and the company (originally called Research In Motion before changing its name to BlackBerry) was acquired by Fairfax Financial. The device still has a devoted cadre of users.

your productivity if even simple calls can take half an hour or more to complete. That all said, relying on a cellphone is a cost-effective option, and if you rely on Internet communication, or even texting, it may be the most appealing option. As with a landline, it might be desirable to get a separate cellphone and cell number for your business.

- *Advantages:* Less expensive option if giving up landline(s) as well. Portability; you can work—or at least communicate with others—from anywhere. Smartphones can give you a large variety of the business tools and services you need in one small device.

- *Disadvantages:* Cell service can be spotty and unreliable. Call quality ranges from acceptable to deplorable. If you talk/text while driving, you are a menace to others on the road—and, in many places, you are breaking the law.

VoIP

Short for "Voice over Internet Protocol," which has come to refer to a wide variety of different types of services that connect telephones—or the equivalent of telephones—over the Internet rather than phone lines or cellular networks. Early VoIP providers like Vonage mimicked the legacy telephone model; a phone connected to the network could call to and receive from any other phone. Later providers like Skype (see Chapter 5) used their own closed networks which meant that you could only use Skype with other registered Skype users.[10] Newer iterations of VoIP have begun to treat phone calling like e-mailing, in that one caller can call any other caller anywhere on the Internet. As we'll point out in Chapter 5, Skype[11] and similar services are the best option if you need to communicate with colleagues or clients overseas, as you

[10] Skype's range of services is expanding, and it is very easy to have conference calls with the program.
[11] The version that comes pre-installed on Windows computers, Dr. Joe has found, is much poorer than the downloadable version.

avoid international call rates which, especially on cellphones, can be extortionate. You can also purchase (for $10) a SkypeIn/Out number in the area code of your choice,[12] and domestic calls are about 2¢ a minute; overseas calls are little more but are still less than calling on a cellphone. You can call to and receive from any landline or cellphone and since Richard has started using this, the call quality (over WiFi) has been almost universally excellent. Calls don't drop, he can hear and be heard by others, and doesn't sound like Charlie Brown's teacher. Skype also has an iPhone (and iPad) app that lets you use your cellphone as...a phone. Take a moment to wrap your head around that.

- *Advantages:* Inexpensive and generally reliable, although Skype does have some issues. Call quality, like that of cellphones, ranges from pretty good to wretched. Skype now has features for multiperson calls, and you can also show your computer screen to the person you have called. You can also get a phone number with an area code of your choice for a limited fee, called "SkypeIn."

- *Disadvantages:* Lack of portability, the Skype app notwith-standing. Spotty call quality, dropped calls. Additional comput-er hardware—microphone and headphones or headset—may be required. Depending on type of VoIP service, you may not be able to communicate with everyone, requiring additional phone service. It is getting better. If you are in a WiFi area with an iPhone or Android phone, the Skype app is quite good.

---

[12] You can obviously pick any area code you like, but it stands to reason you would use the area code in which your office is located. In some places, believe it or not, area codes are something of a status symbol—L.A's 213 and 310, for example—and when there was the big area code expansion and reallocation in the 1990s, some of the more status-conscious among us were none too pleased. This was brilliantly satirized in the *Seinfeld* episode where Elaine has to get a new phone number, but her 212 area code was replaced with 646—and she conspires to hijack her dead neighbor's 212 area code. See http://en.wikipedia.org/wiki/The_Maid_(Seinfeld).

Hanging Online: The E-Mail

Most homes these days have some kind of broadband Internet connectivity, usually through a phone, cable, or other telecommunications company. If it's through your cable company, you will likely have been given a cable modem into which you plug the cable coming into the house. For wireless networks, you simply purchase a wireless router. This device connects to your cable modem and then broadcasts the wireless network signal that is picked up by the computers

Motorola SURFboard cable modem.

and other WiFi-compatible devices in your home, like iPads, iPhones, etc. If you use Apple computers, the router is called an Airport Base Station and can be purchased from the Apple Store online or offline. (Apple Store personnel are pretty knowledgeable and helpful and can readily answer any specific questions about setting up an Airport network.) If you use a PC that runs some version of Windows, you can buy a wireless router at Best Buy, Staples, Walmart, or just about any other big box retailer. Top brands are Netgear, Linksys, and Cisco. They cost, on average, between $50 and $100.

Cable companies like Time-Warner also offer "business class" broadband service that features faster speed and the ability to add

more users. It is, of course, more expensive. For most home businesses, your basic consumer Internet service will suffice, but if your business involves routinely transferring very big files (if

Apple's Airport Extreme (left) and Linksys wireless broadband routers.

you work with video, for example) or you require additional features, you may want to consider upgrading.

It is a sad fact that even today it is not always possible to get broadband Internet service. This is especially the case in rural areas. A freelance graphic designer in a rural part of upstate New

York as recently as 2010 still had no option but to rely on dial-up Internet service, which uses ordinary telephone lines to access the Internet. For those who remember the 1990s, this is painfully slow; fifty-six kilobits per second is the top speed at which phone lines can physically transmit, and few services ever came close to that. By way of comparison, broadband Internet transfer speeds are measured in hundreds of megabits per second (1 megabit = 1,000 kilobits)—some even gigabits (1 gigabit = 1,000 megabits).

If you are stuck with dial-up, your dreams of a home office aren't necessarily dashed. If you get decent cellphone reception and have a high-speed data plan, you may be able to use a tablet computer like an iPad or your smartphone for most of your Internet needs. There are also services like Hightail (formerly YouSendIt) that can be used to transfer large files, allowing you to upload and download them from a central server whenever it is convenient to do so. For example, you may go into town regularly and may be able to access high-speed internet at a coffee shop, restaurant, or public library (see the previous chapter).

In Chapter 6, we will talk about setting up a website, and when you select a web hosting plan and/or purchase a domain, you will also likely get a certain number of e-mail addresses. You should have a single generic e-mail address that potential clients can use for general inquiries and communication, such as info@yourbusiness.com. Then, you can have additional e-mail addresses that get piped to different places, like your own personal address, a sales address, a support address, and so forth, depending on the nature of your business.

If need be, you can always set up a free Gmail address through Google. Gmail addresses are acceptable, and there is little stigma to using them, but an e-mail address that has the "gmail.com" domain will be far less professional than one that has "yourbusiness.com."

But there is an advantage: Gmail can be set up as your regular e-mail software, but the custom domain can send all of its e-mail to you. There can be great advantages to Gmail, so you may find this to be a good option.

"Stabilize" All Your Contact Info ASAP

You obviously want to set up e-mail addresses, phone numbers, and mailing addresses as soon as you can—after all, you want people (like customers) to be able to contact you! And while you can use your residential info at the outset, keep in mind that you will want to produce collateral and promotional materials like business cards, letterhead, envelopes, and mailing labels as soon as you can (see Chapter 6). Even if you don't have a pressing need for letterhead (and fewer and fewer of us do these days), you do need business cards, which should have the correct contact info and should not be "updated" by crossing out an old phone number and writing in the new one by hand.

Therefore, answer the following questions as soon as possible:

- What's your primary business mailing address?
- What's your primary business phone number? Is there also a primary business cellphone number?
- What's your primary business e-mail address?

Moving Forward

This and previous chapters have focused on setting up your business, getting everything in order before you finally open your doors—literally or metaphorically. In the next chapter and beyond, we will look at the mechanics of the actual day-to-day running of the business, starting with how to manage that most precious of commodities: time.

To Do:

❑ Go shopping! Make a list of the furniture, hardware, and software you will need for your home office, and start picking it out. Check out Craigslist or other classified advertising for used office furniture, or search online at, IKEA, for example.

❑ Don't buy too much furniture—prioritize what you buy, and buy less than what you need at first. It's better to start slow and add pieces later.

❑ Experiment with cloud storage or other cloud-based services and software. Get familiar with how they work, if you have not already.

❑ Think about the connectivity trinity: mail, phone, and e-mail. Identify what you want your business mailing address, phone number, and e-mail address to be. Do you want to share it with residential service?

❑ Compare mailbox rates at the Post Office and a third-party location, like The UPS Store. Also consider what types of mail and packages you may be receiving. If you will be receiving a lot of FedEx or UPS packages, a P.O. box may be impractical.

CHAPTER

It's About Time

"Time is an illusion. Lunchtime doubly so."
        —*Douglas Adams, author,* The Hitchhiker's Guide to the Galaxy

"Time flies like an arrow. Fruit flies like a banana."
                —*Groucho Marx, comedian*

Answer These Questions:

Are you a morning person or a night person?

When do you feel at your most productive or efficient?

At what time of day do you function best?

How disciplined are you about work; do you need to be chained to the computer, or do you naturally gravitate to getting work done?

How well do you manage distractions?

How well do you manage time?

All life forms have a natural rhythm, scientifically called "circadian rhythm"[1] which refers to the fact that our biological systems are based on twenty-four-hour cycles. This is why when we travel to different time zones we are so tired and out of it; our bodies are telling us that it's one time, while the clock is telling us that it's another.

Even though we all share the same basic twenty-four-hour rhythm, we all differ in how our functions and activities are distributed in those hours. Some of us are early risers ("morning people") who get up at 5:00 A.M. or so and can jump right into productive work, usually tiring in the late afternoon or early evening and going to bed early. Others are late risers ("night people") who prefer to sleep late in the morning but are productive in the nighttime hours, starting in the late afternoon and working productively until midnight or even  later—or earlier, depending on how you want to look at it. We don't often choose this rhythm, but whether through habit, biology, the schedules of the people around us, psychology, or some combination of these factors, it chooses us.[2] When we have a nine-to-five office job, the hours we are required to be at work can collide with our natural tendency, whether it means we are habitually late or grumpy until mid-morning or run out of steam after three in the afternoon.

[1] See http://en.wikipedia.org/wiki/Circadian_rhythm.
[2] Scientists have found some genetic basis for the "morning person"; see http://abcn.ws/TzjdJX.

None to Five: Tailoring a Work Schedule

With a home business, however, it can be easier to tailor a work schedule so that it is more compatible with our biological tendency. Depending on what it is we do and the extent to which we need to be available to colleagues or clients, we may not be able to *completely* conform to our biological rhythm. If you're a night person and happen to be a sales rep, no one is going to be too happy about you making sales calls at two in the morning, unless your client is in China. Likewise, if you need to connect with clients, you need to be available when they are up and about and at work.[3]

Some people have the luxury—if that's what you want to call it—of not having to interact with colleagues in real time at all. We once worked with a data analyst who tended to work overnight, and files would be e-mailed at three or four in the morning. He was never available during the day, but he didn't need to be. He got his work done efficiently and, in fact, it worked out more conveniently for his coworkers who were not waiting around during the day for files to be e-mailed.

Sometimes, though, we can split the difference. Writers, designers, and others who need to concentrate intently on specific projects find it easier to get those tasks done in the early morning or late night hours because there are fewer interruptions and distractions. The phone doesn't ring, there are fewer instant messagers or texters up and around (unless we work with other morning or night people), and visitors are unlikely to show up at our door. With the bulk of work being done either early in the morning or late at night, we can do low-level tasks and be available to callers during the nine-to-five period.

When you first start out working from home, you will need to experiment to see what your natural rhythm is. Some of us have been able to find our internal clock while still working in an out-

---

[3] E-mail helps solve some of this problem. If your business communication can stand a little time lag, it may be acceptable for people to send you notes during *their* "normal" business hours and for you to respond during *your* "normal" business hours.

side office, if we were lucky enough to have flexible schedules and could often go into work at more biologically convenient hours.

You probably already know, or at least have a sense, of what your own rhythm is, but a good way to discover it is to spend a couple of days waking, working, and sleeping unaided. Go to bed when you're sleepy, wake up when you wake up without setting the alarm clock, and work when you feel naturally disposed to it.[4] Two or three days spent in this way will likely uncover your own natural rhythm.

One fly in this particular ointment is that your natural rhythm may collide with others in your household, and you may have rea-

sons other than work to operate on a more conventional schedule. The kids may need to get off to school, the spouse may have to go to work at a certain time, and the cat, dog, fruit bat, etc., may function as furry alarm clocks. So although you may not be

entirely able to set your own schedule, a little experimenting should allow you to strike a comfortable balance for you to get the contiguous blocks of time that you need.

TELECOMMUTING

If you telecommute to a main office rather than run your own home business, you will probably be at the mercy of the company's operating hours. Managers, coworkers, and clients may expect you to be on call during those hours, and you may get penalized or fired if you vary your schedule or fail to be available when needed. After all, telecommuting is not an excuse to play hooky. You may not have the luxury of making your own hours, but mobile technology can help increase your availability to others while at the same time letting you operate on a schedule that is more conducive to your own

---

[4] Be careful not to miss deadlines, meetings, scheduled calls, etc., of course. And if you *never* feel naturally disposed to working, perhaps working at home is not for you.

internal productivity. Most telecommuting arrangements involve a commitment to always be available during certain hours of the day, such as from 10:00 A.M. to 3:00 P.M., with the other hours left flexible.

DON'T BECOME A SLAVE TO YOUR SCHEDULE

On the down side, becoming slaves to our own internal schedules can keep us from being productive on demand. For example, you may get your best writing done at 6:00 A.M., with 2:00 P.M. being your least productive period. But if you get a 2:00 P.M. call from a client or coworker requiring something to be written "immediately," you can't beg out and respond, "This is a down time for me. It'll be better if I do it tomorrow morning." That's simply not going to fly.

So, yes, develop your own productive schedule, but make sure that it is a strong but flexible preference.

Time Passages: Filtering Distractions

While we want or need to make ourselves available, sometimes we can make ourselves *too* available.

A lot of working at home is about managing time, and most of managing time is creating effective filters for the things that can take time away from our productive work. Visitors, phone calls, instant messages, e-mail, social media—all of these things can intrude on us when we need to be accomplishing tasks.

Most of us are very bad at filtering out distractions. We immediately drop everything if the phone rings or the text message application chimes. As soon as new e-mail arrives, we jump over to our e-mail program and read it. We have our instant messaging and social media applications open and immediately respond to messages or status updates. As the number of ways to communicate has increased, so, too, has the number of ways we can be distracted.

The reason we are bad at filtering out distractions is largely psychological. We may fear we are missing something vital if we let that call go to voicemail, or if we turn the instant messaging program off, or if we don't check e-mail every five seconds. And now with Twitter, if we're not "part of the conversation," we may as well not exist, apparently. And while, yes, that *may* be true in certain circumstances (maybe we are expecting an important call or are waiting for a response to something), the fact is that more than—arguably—seventy-five percent of the time, any given communication is not vitally urgent and will keep if left unchecked for a short period of time.

In fact, it's not unusual to welcome these distractions as a way to deliberately avoid working on something we really don't want to work on, or something we are having trouble getting started on. We all have tasks or projects like that; the house is never cleaner, the yard never more manicured, than when there is a project we are putting off. It's a hard pill to swallow, but working at home demands discipline.

We should not be afraid to "uncommunicate" at certain times. It's often the only way that we can manage our productivity. It can even be desirable, particularly when working on deadline or an important project, to go completely dark, or enter "Fortress of Solitude"[5] mode: you turn the phone(s) off, you quit the e-mail program, you turn off Skype and instant messaging, and put up the "do not disturb" sign you came up with (see Chapter 2).

While encasing oneself in an ice fortress like Superman may be a little extreme, the principle is sound.

Some people have strategies for allowing important people to get in touch in emergencies while keeping out potential distractions and time sinks. Some splurge on private phone lines or cell numbers that are only given out to important people with instructions that they are only to be used in emergencies. Then they know they can turn off the other commu-nication routes. Caller ID and customized ringtones are also good filters to help keep the distractions out. Some people use a super secret instant messaging screen name[6] that they only give out to those VIPs. When you need privacy, only log on with that name.

---

[5] See http://en.wikipedia.org/wiki/Fortress_of_solitude. In upstate New York in winter, the similarities increase.
[6] Or Skype name, etc.

The Death of the Autoresponder

If we had been writing this book as recently as four or five years ago, we would likely have discussed in the main text the pros and cons of using an "autoresponder." This is an automated "out-of-office" message generator that automatically responds to incoming e-mails when you don't have access to it. We used to see these a lot, but as more and more people started using smartphones, they became unnecessary, and now it almost seems as if there is a kind of stigma attached to using an autoresponder. The expectation is that you have access to e-mail wherever you are, which may or may not be true. If you telework, corporate policy may limit your ability to check company e-mail on a mobile device, which may be a good thing. But if you are self-employed or are in other ways entrepreneurial, you may have no choice but to ditch the autoresponder— even if you really can't check e-mail remotely. If you must use an autoresponder, don't be afraid to set up the autoresponder to include a link to your Web site or your latest white paper, or some very brief marketing message.

Respond When Required

When applying filters, we need to be careful not to become too blasé about incoming communication. While most e-mail or phone messages can wait, they can't wait too long, otherwise we forget about them. How many times have you received an e-mail that required a response, put off actually composing that response, and as new messages came in, that message gradually moved down your mailbox until it disappeared off the screen. Once that happens, it's gone. And then three days later you get a snarky follow-up message asking why you ignored the first message.[7]

If this has happened to you, you are not alone. We are inundated with communication, and it is easy to forget about an e-mail or a voicemail. One solution is to block out a certain period of time where you will only check e-mail or voicemail, and then in that period make it a point to attend to everything that requires a response. That may be easier said than done, but it's worth trying.

---

[7] Depending on how well our mobile devices are synced with our main computers, sometimes we get a message on a mobile device, plan to respond at a more propitious time, and then forget about it because the message did not appear in our computer's mailbox.

THE PROS AND CONS OF MULTITASKING

The tendency to do several different things at the same time can also complicate our time management issues. While talking on the phone, we might be composing an e-mail, while at the same time instant messaging, while trying to write a press release *and* update our social media status. Is it any wonder that many messages are badly garbled, poorly worded, and/or ill-conceived?

Now, some people *like* multitasking, usually because they are quite good at it. Younger adults are especially proficient, probably because they grew up as all these communication technologies were emerging. Multitasking is second nature to them. It's not for everyone, though, and one of the important aspects of finding our natural rhythm is finding out the extent to which we can multitask effectively. Once we determine how many balls we can have in the air at a time, we can apply filters to the others.

Setting Office Hours

Once you have found and established your natural rhythm, you will need to convey those hours to others, especially those in your household. This is related to the "do not disturb" sign we discussed in Chapter 2: tell your spouse, children, and/or other cohabitants what your office hours are, when it's okay to be disturbed, and when it's not. As for off-site colleagues or clients, you can discuss it with them on an individual basis. Not everyone you work with may need to know your schedule, but if you collaborate closely with anyone, you may want to drop them a note telling

TMI

Be careful about giving out too much information about your schedule. It's really no one's business that you're picking up the kids, or are at the gym. You can tell people "I reserve 3 P.M. to 4 P.M. for retainer conference calls." No one needs to know what you're *really* doing. Always guard your time with a business reason. This is not because we like being sneaky and secretive (although we do), but because there is still a negative connotation to working at home, that you're just "goofing off" or shirking work, and you don't want to reinforce that perception.

them that "I am usually 'out to lunch' from 11:30 A.M. to 12:30 P.M." or whatever you decide is your break time. Most of your colleagues will be able to figure it out, especially if you use the status messages in an instant messager and/or Skype (see Chapter 5) to let your contacts know if you are available or unavailable. After a while, people will begin to figure out your schedule—probably even better than you know it!

BE STRICT

Setting office hours becomes a pointless exercise if we are not strict about enforcing them. This is especially the case where children are concerned, as they can insist on wanting to play or require some other attention while you are trying to work. The only real solution is to exert parental authority. The same goes for spouses or other cohabitants.

Insomnia Is Nothing to Lose Sleep Over

One would think that by checking e-mail right before bed, and then again first thing in the morning, there would not be any pressing messages waiting, just marketing pitches, spam, and other bulk e-mail. And yet, once in a while, you do get a note from someone that came in at three in the morning. Obviously, someone had insomnia, and thought they would get a little work done. (We've also known people that use the 3:00 A.M. e-mail as a passive-aggressive way of demonstrating how overworked they are.)

When you have a home office, it's easy to not let sleeplessness go to waste. While it is certainly not desirable, and you shouldn't make a habit out of it, the odd bout of insomnia can be put to reasonably productive use.

There is also the insomnia that is brought about by waking up abruptly with a great idea for a project you are working on. As we all know, sometimes the solutions to problems come to us when our minds are occupied elsewhere, which is why we occasionally wake up with those "Eureka!" moments. And experience has taught us to act on those moments, or, like dreams, will be scarcely remembered come dawn.

Some of us use insomnia to accomplish various tasks. Even without getting up and turning on the computer, sometimes we can strategize, conceptualize, and organize. It certainly beats obsessing about negative thoughts and other troubles (real or imagined), that will be there in the morning.

The flipside is also worth noting. If you had a "real" job you did not like, you may have figured out that insomnia was caused by worrying about that job. Insomnia may disappear once you start working at home because you can have a greater sense of control about your work life and your schedule.

Moving Forward

Once you have learned what your natural rhythm is, and what work schedule best fits that rhythm, and you have communicated your office hours—directly or indirectly—to all those concerned, it's time to start working...and collaborating. While you may choose to work from home to be free of distractions, chances are you will need to occasionally need to talk to someone. In the next chapter, we'll show you how.

To Do:

❑ Determine what time(s) of day are your most productive. Find out when you are most alert and focused and the least sluggish. To the best of your ability, given your specific household circumstances, set these times as your office hours.

❑ Tell the other members of your household what these hours are, and that you should not be interrupted—unless it's an emergency—during those times. Also make sure you have the "do not disturb" sign at the ready should something come up that requires you to enter "Fortress of Solitude" mode.

❑ If it is necessary, communicate your work schedule to colleagues or collaborators. It might be best to phrase this as "best times to reach me" rather than "this is when I am working."

CHAPTER **5**

"I Want to Be Alone"

"Loneliness is everything it's cracked up to be."
> —Alan Alda, TV and movie actor

"I never said, 'I want to be alone.' I only said, 'I want to be let alone.' There is a world of difference."
> —Greta Garbo, movie actress

Answer These Questions:

How do you typically communicate—or plan to communicate—with colleagues? Exclusively by phone or e-mail? Instant messaging? Skype?

If you need to have a conference call, how would you do it?

If you need to conduct a Web conference, or give a "virtual" presentation, would you know how to set it up?

How do you plan to get new clients?

How good are you at business networking? What networking events do you attend, or would like to attend?

Do you have an "elevator speech" about your business?

Regardless of the business you're in, chances are you will need to interact with *someone* at some point. No one works in a vacuum except astronauts, and even they are always interacting with Mission Control. If you're a writer, you need to communicate with editors/publishers, co-authors, and the people you are actually writing *for*. Even if you self-publish and/or write a blog that you update yourself, you will still occasionally find yourself interacting with the people who have bought your writing or those who have commented on your blog post. Most businesses also have (or *should* have) customers and clients. If yours doesn't, well, that's a serious problem.

> ## Many Choices
>
> In this age of myriad communication technologies, people have preferences for how they like to connect. Each of us prefers one particular medium over another. Your clients will each have their own preferences, and other colleagues will also have their chosen channels. Is it phone? Text? E-mail? Skype? As a service provider, you will need to understand how each of your clients or other colleagues prefer to stay in touch and adapt accordingly. You may hate being called on the phone, but still realize that some people prefer it and thus never check e-mail. And vice versa. We need to be adaptable.

In Chapter 3, we discussed the Connectivity Trinity, or the three primary means of business communication—mail, phone, and e-mail—but in this chapter we'll focus on the other ways we can interact and collaborate with colleagues and/or clients.

Informal Interaction

The telephone is, obviously, a great way to communicate, but it isn't always efficient. Let's say you need to know when a meeting is scheduled. You could call and ask, but that can involve the dreaded "phone tag" or balloon into a lengthy phone conversation. Sending text messages is a great way to efficiently ask simple questions and get simple responses. Still, there can be some lag in the response. Not everyone has texting capabilities, and some wireless customers still get charged high rates for text messages, so they often prefer to limit them.

A simple—and free—solution is instant messaging (IM). It works essentially like texting on a cellphone[1]: you send short messages to people in your contacts list (some services call this a "Buddy List"). Instant messaging works either on a computer or on any mobile device, depending on the specific IM application you use.

Texting is a nice, quick way to get simple answers, confirm appointments, and give status updates.

There are many programs out there for instant messaging, and hardcore IM nerds can easily recommend their favorite highly obscure programs. On the Macintosh, iChat comes with the OS, and is the default messaging program. It works like—and closely resembles—the Messages app that is used for texting on an iPhone. In newer versions of the Mac, you can use iChat to send text messages from your computer to a mobile phone.

On Windows, there have been some changes over the years, but current versions of Windows encourage you to use the chat/texting feature in Skype for instant messaging. And, in fact, more and more people are in fact using Skype.

There is no shortage of third-party instant messaging applications, such as Adium, Pidgin, and many more that let you access one or more instant messaging networks. These networks—like AOL Instant Messenger (AIM), Google Messenger, and others—are important in order to connect with others. If you have an account on AIM, you may not be able to IM with someone who is on Google, or vice versa. Therefore, it is important that whatever IM program you use be compatible with whatever networks your contacts are on,

---

[1] Actually, cellphone texting is based on the same principles as instant messaging, which predated texting.

Chat with drjwwebb

8:35 AM

I am sending you a message.

I would send a response but I'm too lazy.

Had this been an actual message, it would have contained information.

I'm tired of your half breed interference Mr Spock.

Fascinating.

I don't know if the warp engines can take it, Captain

Damn it, Jim, I'm a doctor not an engineer!

Choo choo Charlie was an engineer

Instant messaging is a convenient way to collaborate remotely. You can see how productive IM conversations can be.

otherwise you will just be talking to yourself.[2]

If you are a teleworking employee, your parent company will likely tell you what program and network to use for messaging, and they may also have their own corporate network. It's actually not uncommon for managers to randomly message teleworkers to make sure, Big Brother-like, that they are actually at their desks.

As we pointed out in the last chapter, it can be useful—if not necessary—to turn off your instant messaging every once in a while, particularly if you are deeply immersed in a task that requires intense concentration, like writing a book about teleworking. Sometimes, whenever the incoming message chime sounds, one has a tendency to tell oneself, "There goes productivity." Still, it may be important and even crucial to have that constant connectivity.

SOCIAL MEDIA

Unless you have been locked in an underwater pyramid for the past five years, you have probably encountered the term "social media," or at the very least seen references to Facebook, LinkedIn, and Twitter, and maybe one or two others (Instagram, Pinterest). It is a broad generalization to say that they are all basically different versions of the same thing—ways of networking with others via the Internet—but they have some important distinctions. Those distinctions will become more important in the Chapter 6 when

---

[2] IM programs will, in fact, let you send messages to yourself. We don't recommend doing this, although, as the old joke about talking to yourself goes, sometimes it's the only way to have an intelligent conversation.

we discuss using these sites for promoting your business. For the basics of networking, here is what you need to know about each of the Big Three social media sites:

Facebook

Facebook wasn't originally designed to be a business networking site or tool; it was intended more for keeping in touch with friends and family. However, Facebook has become more business-friendly over the years, and today offers many ways to promote your business. We will look at this in slightly more detail in Chapter 6, but you can get a start at https://www.facebook.com/business.

Now, whether you use Facebook for personal or business purposes—or both—depends on with whom you connect. If you only connect with colleagues and talk business, then it's a business-oriented profile. If you only link to friends and family and share pictures of kids, pets, or meals, then it is personal. Most of us use Facebook for some combination of business and personal, with an emphasis on the latter. And of course many people avoid it entirely, and they are not wrong to do so.

Anti-Social Media?

It's tempting to think that only older people or Luddites avoid Facebook, but many younger people now choose not to be on it (what kid wants to hang out on the same social media as his parents?), but even twenty- and thirtysomethings are giving it a pass. One of our young WhatTheyThink colleagues—one of the most technologically astute people we know—is not on social media at all.

Remember, though, that managers and other colleagues can see what you are up to on Facebook—and many do in fact keep tabs on teleworkers that way—so be careful what you post. If you are supposed to be hard at work, and you post pictures of yourself at the beach (posts are time- and location-stamped), don't be surprised if you get some sort of admonition.

Facebook is a good tool for basic interaction; it has different types of messaging, too, so you can use it as an e-mail or even instant messaging program, which is convenient if you like to keep everything self-contained in one site.

We'll look at the business uses of Facebook in the Chapter 6.

LinkedIn

LinkedIn can be described as "Facebook for business." It has many of the same features as Facebook, but it is intended for business connections and networking. Again, we'll look at LinkedIn in more detail in the Chapter 6, but for now, LinkedIn is where you go to talk business and not post pictures of your dinner.  One of the most important aspects of LinkedIn is the Groups, where you join specific discussions related to your business and industry.

Like Facebook, there is a general newsfeed, where you post status updates, projects you have worked on and completed, awards or acknowledgements you have received, and links to and comments on stories related to your field. There is also an extensive job board, and LinkedIn is fast becoming the way that job seekers and potential employers connect. If you are running your own home business, that may not interest you, but you should be aware of that feature.

LinkedIn Pulse is a new place to blog (we have used it), and it's a good place to re-use old blog posts. In the next chapter we will look at some of the new capabilities that LinkedIn offers, from easy-to-create web pages spun off from LinkedIn profiles to mini-presentations via LinkedIn's acquisition of Slideshare.

Twitter

Perhaps the best way to think about Twitter is as being akin to the news crawls that scroll along the bottom of cable news channel screens. The writer has only 140 characters in which to convey a message, which will be little more than a headline. Typically, there is also a link to a longer comment or article. Many people do use it for direct messaging, although conversations are visible to all your and your correspondents' followers. This can be a little confusing if you only follow one side of the conversation. Twitter has also become one of the chief customer relations tools used by businesses—or, we should say, by the customers of businesses—be they large or small. Customer inquiries and complaints are increasingly being funneled through Twitter. Also, businesses are being talked *about*, in the third person, on Twitter and elsewhere in the social media universe. As a result, you need to know what people may be saying about you.

Social media certainly has its advantages, both as a tool for networking and as a means of marketing and promoting one's business. However, a chainsaw is also a tool, and movies like *The Texas Chainsaw Massacre* show us how a tool can be misused. Likewise, it can be too easy to become addicted to social media and spend all one's time on Facebook or Twitter doing little that is productive or useful. Of course, television, radio, music, books, and the Internet in general have long provided the same types of distractions and diversions. It sometimes takes a great deal of discipline to turn these things off when there is work to be done.

Three's Company—Or, Don't Come and Knock On Our Door

Many people who work from home are relieved of the obligation to attend meetings, which are the bane of many traditional office workers. They are productivity killing at best and soul destroying at worst. However, in some cases (and the percentage is open to debate), they are a necessary conduit for collaboration. When we pick up new clients or projects, it's often necessary to assemble the team that will be working on the project to outline objectives, identify deliverables, milestones, and due dates, and assign specific tasks. Meetings may also be needed sporadically throughout the life of a project to track progress, answer questions, and solve problems.

For work-at-home types, these types of meetings are often held via conference call. The term "conference call" implies that a number of participants are in on a group telephone call, but today there are a variety of different ways a "conference call" can be held.

CONFERENCE BY PHONE

This is the traditional definition of a conference call. You pick up your telephone, dial into a conference call hosting service, enter a conference number, and you are joined with other people who have called in.

The simplest way of hosting a conference call is by using the "conferencing" or "three- (or more) way calling" feature of many telephones or telephone plans. A host conferences in participants from their phone. The drawbacks include only being able to conference in a small number of people (three is usually the maximum), extra phone company charges for its use, and, perhaps most importantly, the rise of cellular communications. Although some cell plans and phones offer conferencing or three-way calling, it's an imperfect solution for larger conferencing needs.

> ### In Our Experience: The Ins and Outs
>
> We cannot stress often enough that if you're using a cellphone as your primary business phone, make sure you have decent reception. It can be frustrating, and irritating for others on the call, when a conference participant is constantly getting disconnected and has to re-dial-in. We've had better luck calling into conference calls using Skype and a headset. The quality is much better than a volatile cell connection. Usually. Sometimes Skype has bad days.

Many large companies have their own conference call hosting systems that allow both in-house and remote workers to call into a central number. One person sets up the conference call and arranges to have the dial-in information sent to participants. At call time, everyone dials in to the central number, enters a numerical code for the conference and, once the host has arrived, is placed into conference. There are sound cues that indicate when a participant has joined or left the conference.

The easiest way to participate in a conference call is to simply dial into someone else's conference call system. But what if *you* have to be the host of a conference call without having access to a conference calling system? Wouldn't installing one cost a lot of money? As it happens, just about everyone has access to free conference calling via a service named, cleverly enough, FreeConferenceCall.com.

With FreeConferenceCall, you sign up for a free account online simply by entering a user name and password. Once you have an account, you can reserve a date and time for a conference call, and you'll be given a dial-in number[3] and an access code. You can invite up to ninety-six participants, and calls can last as long as six hours. It's available 24/7, and there is no limit to the number of free conference calls you can schedule. The service also includes free call recording and other features. The call quality is generally very good and the service is reliable. We have used FreeConferenceCall for a number of our own projects and have never had a problem with it.

FreeConferenceCall also has for-pay plans that offer toll-free calling (if some of your participants are far-flung and long-distance charges are likely to be high) and some that offer screen sharing for online meetings, if you need to include a visual presentation. FreeConferenceCall has been offering more in the way of web conferencing services lately.

Ambient Noise

When you are on a conference call, be sure to reduce the ambient or background noise as much as possible in order to a) not distract the meeting and b) to convey professionalism. You should not have the TV or music on in the background, the children should be out of earshot, and pets, too, should be secreted away. This is why we stress the importance of an office door. Unless you can't avoid it, schedule calls for when these conditions are possible. Sometimes all you need to say is "these are the times I am available" to avoid these problems. As we pointed out earlier in this book, also leave a note on the door for mail carriers, UPS and FedEx, and other potential unannounced visitors. Also don't overlook using the "Mute" button when necessary.

---

[3] While there is no cost to set up the conference call, participants may incur long-distance call charges.

Skype also has conference call capabilities, and one of its benefits is the "show screen" feature that allows others on Skype to see a presenter's computer desktop, such as a Word, Excel, or PowerPoint file or other files (more about this later).

There is also a service called Speek (www.speek.com) that takes conference calling to the next level, integrating teleconferencing with a browser or a mobile app to let you see who has joined or left a call, chat, share files, and record the call.

CONFERENCE BY VIDEO

Today, videoconferencing is pretty much synonymous with Skype and FaceTime, but there are a number of different videoconferencing applications on the market.

All the Office's a Stage...

When videoconferencing, pay attention to what is visible to the webcam. Our home offices can be our private domains, but think about the impression you are conveying to others if you have a messy desk or inappropriate wall décor. Look around your office location and make sure your webcam "studio" space is presentable. (Skype, for example, shows you what your webcam is broadcasting, making it easy to see if there is anything behind you that should be hidden.) Also check lighting; sometimes our general office lighting is not enough for a webcam to broadcast a bright image, and sometimes directional desk lamps can create strange, often macabre, effects.

Now, we say "videoconferencing," but Skype can be used just like any other audio-only conference calling service. Indeed, you can turn the video off, if you are not in a presentable enough state to be seen by other professionals. Skype can be used for conference-calling purposes, as above: the host manually conferences in other Skype users or even participants with outside phone numbers.

Larger companies may also have their own videoconferencing systems, which can be accessed via computer.

If you have a Google account, Google Hangouts (https://hangouts.google.com) is a good videoconferencing option, as well. It does take some setting up and troubleshooting, so if you have a "Hangout" scheduled and you've

Skype has become synonymous with video calls, which are free between and among Skype users.

not used it before, be sure to log on 10 or 15 minutes in advance to make sure everything is working.

Whether you use Skype or some other videoconferencing tool, you will need a computer equipped with a microphone and a web-cam.[4] Many computers these days come with webcams (Apple Mac-Book notebook computers have long come with built-in webcams standard), but if not they can be purchased at Best Buy and else-where for as low as $25, more for HD webcams. Most external web-cams also include built-in microphones. Tablet computers like iPads and other mobile devices now come with cameras and microphones, allowing you to use these devices for video conferencing as well.

The trick with Skype and/or other video conferencing can be getting your A/V hardware—camera and microphone—working with the system so that you can be both seen and heard. It's advisable to log on up to fifteen minutes before the start of your video conference to troubleshoot any A/V issues. Although everyone is aware of the occasional flakiness of modern technology, it still gives you a more professional appearance if you are ready to go right at the appointed start of a videoconference.

There is one great advantage to videoconferencing: attendees

---

[4] Skype also has an app for the iPhone, iPad, Android, and other mobile devices.

tend to be on their best behavior. Because they know others can see them, they are less likely to be answering e-mail or surfing the Internet while on the call. There is a noticeable increase in engagement with videoconferences.

CONFERENCE BY WEB

Conference calls are nice, relatively low-tech ways of collaborating and meeting, and videoconferencing is good for being "almost there." But often, we need to have virtual meetings in which we share information, usually in presentation form. We can do this through either of the other two channels, of course: you can e-mail everyone a PowerPoint or a PDF file and, on a traditional conference call, walk participants through the presentation by saying, "Turn to Slide 3." In many ways, that solves many of the technical problems that can arise with web conferencing systems.

But for those who do need to host or participate in web conferences, there are many ways of accomplishing it.

Skype lets users share their screens, facilitating webconferencing and remote presentations

At the simplest level, Skype has a "share this screen" feature, which works remarkably well. For simple web conferencing, this may be all you need. You conference in Skype users (naturally, this won't work if you are conferencing in anyone on a telephone), and as long as one of the people you are conferencing with has Skype Premium, you—or anyone on the call—can share your screen.

Many large companies have their own web conferencing solutions, and if you are merely a participant, you simply use your computer to login using the access information your host will provide. As with videoconferencing, there may be some technical glitches, depending on the computer you are using and the extent to which it is compatible with the hosting system. We again advise to log on a few minutes beforehand for any troubleshooting.

If you need to host a web conference, and Skype won't work for you, there are a variety of options, including (but not limited to):

- *Anymeeting.* A popular web conferencing service for small businesses, and although they have a free version that can support up to 200 participants, it includes ads, which may not convey the kind of professionalism you need. They do have various ad-free, for-pay options that support more participants. Compare their plans at www.anymeeting.com.

- *WebEx.* Cisco's web conferencing utility. They have a variety of plans, ranging from free (up to three participants, standard-definition video only) to $89 per month (one hundred people per meeting, up to nine hosts, high-definition video). See their plans compared at www.webex.com/plans/meetings-plans.html.

- *GoToMeeting.* One of the most popular web conferencing solutions available, although it does not offer a free version. (They do offer a one-month free trial though.) They have plans starting at $49 a month (up to twenty-five participants), and higher-level plans offer the ability to add participants, use various "audience management" tools, and take advantage of other features. Compare their plans at www.gotomeeting. com/fec/web_conferencing_comparison.[5]

- *Zoom*. A service that enables up to 25 HD video feeds. An upgrade from the basic version is available for conducting professional meetings, seminars, and other events that need to be managed well. It supports any device, and costs $9.99 a month or $99.00 a year. Users have told us they even prefer it to Skype. Check it out at www.zoom.us.

The drawback to these is that most require a subscription, which is good if you host a lot of web conferences but can be a waste of money if you only need to host one occasionally. One solution may be to go in on a subscription plan with other colleagues or businesses you know. As long as you don't all schedule a meeting for the same time, it could be an effective solution.

These "virtual meeting" applications integrate with Twitter and other social media, which can be useful if the content of the meeting is designed for public consumption, like a Webinar.

Try It Before You Buy It

Many of these tele-, video-, and web conferencing options have a free trial period. Take advantage of these to compare and contrast how the different systems work and which you think would be a good fit for your business needs. If the free trial isn't missing any essential features or has other severe limits, save the trial for an actual conference. That's the best way to test the extent to which it meets your needs.

Networking Opportunities in the Wild

Depending on where you live and work, there may be ample opportunities to connect with others out in the "real world" or "meetspace" (or perhaps "meatspace") as some call it. Networking events are excellent opportunities to meet potential clients or customers or just meet others in the community. Not everyone likes

---

[5] The other services that Citrix offers, such as GoToWebinar and GoToMyPC, can be quite valuable for offering a good professional impression.

networking, and not everyone is especially good at it. If you are running your own business, however, it's a vital skill to develop.

Any party or gathering is essentially a networking event, but here are some business-specific venues for networking.

CHAMBERS OF COMMERCE

One of first networking actions you may want to consider when starting your home-based business is to join your local Chamber of Commerce. Chambers of Commerce differ in what they offer members, but the best of them provide a variety of resources for local businesses including:

- special educational seminars and events, such as how to use social media for business marketing
- saving money on health insurance, electricity, and other products and services
- referrals from other Chamber members
- member news in Chamber print and online publications
- networking events

Many Chambers of Commerce also serve as local district chapters of the Small Business Association (SBA).

Although there are many advantages to joining the local Chamber, one primary advantage is networking. Many have regular (i.e., monthly) networking events. There are also occasional breakfasts and lunches, all of which provide ample networking opportunities.

TRADE EVENTS

Depending on the industry in which you work, chances are there is some big trade event where vendors and customers meet and network with each other. These are great opportunities to meet new faces, collect business cards, and get your name and face out among potential clients.

How do you find trade events? There are likely one or more trade publications (in print or online) that serve your industry, and

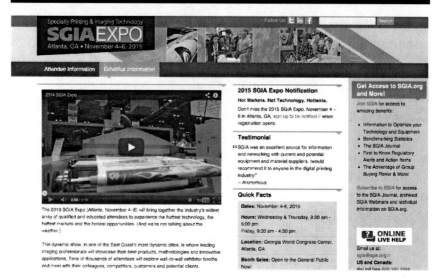

Major trade events in your industry can be excellent networking opportunities. In our industry, the SGIA Expo show is held annually and draws tens of thousands of people from around the U.S. to see the latest in specialty graphics printing.

these publications include calendars of events. Depending on your industry, there may be a wide variety of events, and they may be far-flung. Choosing which industry event(s) to attend will be a function of your travel budget, time available, and perceived return on investment. Maybe your industry's big annual conference is being held in Dubai this year. Are you likely to get enough new business to justify the expense of traveling there? A smaller, closer-to-home event may be more practical, especially if you have not attended a trade event before.

You may even achieve a certain level of renown in your business so that you are invited to speak or take part in panel discussions at industry trade events, and your own presentations can be excellent promotional opportunities. However, unless you have a great desire to be a professional paid speaker, you may have to pick and choose these events. After all, travel is disruptive and can take time away from your primary business. And getting on a plane every other week is worse than commuting to an office every day!

Seven Networking Tips for Introverts

Not everyone is a slick salesman, and many of us are not predisposed to walking into a room full of strangers and chatting people up. Some of us are true "introverts," but even very mild introversion doesn't help navigate social situations. If you are decidedly not the extrovert, here are some tips for getting the most out of networking events.

1. Arrive early, ideally within the first fifteen or twenty minutes of the event, when the crowd is still somewhat sparse and attendees haven't settled into more or less permanent groups or cliques (or "bouquets," as Tom Wolfe once described it). You will likely be more comfortable approaching individuals rather than groups.

2. Go in with an achievable objective or a goal, such as "I am going to meet five new people or collect five new business cards."

3. Don't overreach. Don't expect that you will land five major new clients and sign contracts on the spot. Networking events are about making initial connections that may bear fruit at some point in the future. Follow-up is where the *real* action is.

4. Develop a list of questions or topics beforehand. Often the best way to make a good impression on others is to let them talk, listen attentively, and ask questions. So draw up a list of questions or topics beforehand to get the conversation started. Just don't pull any topic cards out of your pocket. Easy "icebreakers" can simply involve the event or the venue ("Looks like a good turnout," "Do you come to many of these events?" "I love this restaurant; have you ever eaten here?" etc.). "Tell me about your business" is another good way to let the other person start talking.

5. Prepare and rehearse your "elevator speech" (see sidebar later in this chapter), your thumbnail verbal description of your business. You'd be surprised how tongue-tied we become when we are asked to talk about our own business!

6. Stand in line. Queuing up for the buffet, the bar, or the bathroom often provides a captive audience—the person in front of you and/or the person behind you. Take advantage of that situation.

7. If you think you might be interested in having a long-term membership with this organization, volunteering for committees or events is the best way to meet people because you will share a common goal. You will meet others in the natural course of working the registration table or planning the events. The interactions are more natural, and you have to worry less about "opening lines" or meaningless chatter.

You can often find out what trade events are coming to your town by visiting the website of your local convention center. There may be a big expo in your line of business coming to town.

TRADE ASSOCIATIONS

Most professions have at least one professional association or organization that serves a variety of functions, from offering training and educational materials for member companies and individuals, to running trade shows, to serving as "experts" for the media, to promoting a particular industry, to lobbying local, state, and federal governments, and more. Some of the most visible associations are entities such as the American Medical Association (AMA), the American Bar Association (ABA), the Motion Picture Association of America (MPAA), and the National Association of Realtors (NAR). Lesser known trade asso-

The "Elevator Speech"

Any businessperson—whether running a home business or not—should have a so-called "elevator speech" tucked away in his/her back pocket (figuratively, not literally). An elevator speech is a short summary of your business and is essentially a sales pitch. The term derives from the scenario wherein you are riding an elevator and you have thirty to sixty seconds to answer the question, "So what do you do?". We often give short shrift to the elevator speech (also called an elevator pitch) but it should be one of the first things you develop when you set up your business. In fact, it's often the *one* thing that will sell you and your company to a potential client, and, like business cards, is something you should never leave the office without.

How do you write an effective elevator speech? Start by answering each of these questions.

1. Who are you? *"I am a _____..."*

2. What do you do? *"...who does _____..."*

3. Who are your clients? *"...for _____..."*

4. Why should someone hire you? *"...because I can _____. ..."*

5. What do you want to happen next? *"I'd be happy to set up a time to discuss _____..."*

6. How can you conclude with a catchy "hook"? *"Don't you wish you could*
_____*? Don't you wish there were someone who could help you with*
_____*?"*

7. Put it all together.

That's half the battle right there. Now, here are six tips for presenting the elevator speech:

1. Keep it short. It's not an escalator or a five-story walk-up speech. The Delete key is your friend when you are crafting an elevator pitch. It should be short and punchy—lasting no longer than thirty or sixty seconds at the most. Remember; if you are talking with someone, they will ask follow-up questions if they're interested, so there's no need to cram every detail about your business into the speech.

2. Avoid jargon and "corporate speak." When we work in specific industries, we often use special terminology as a kind of shorthand when communicating with colleagues. Remember that someone outside your industry may have no idea what you're talking about, so try to use plain language. Also, avoid corporatespeak words like "synergy," "core competency," and so forth. It should sound natural coming from you, not from a company press release.

3. Practice it out loud and memorize it. Writing a speech and delivering it orally are two completely different things. What reads great on paper may sound stilted and unnatural when spoken. So make sure you practice it out loud before taking it on the road. And don't be afraid to try it out on family, friends, or close colleagues. Be sure to listen carefully to feedback and advice. Also be sure to memorize it; you don't want to be at a social event and have to read it off an index card.

4. Be passionate. Conveying a passion and an enthusiasm for your business is a must. If you sound blasé, uninterested, or modest about your own business, how can you expect anyone else to be interested in it?

5. Have several versions. Different audiences and venues require different approaches, and it's vital to target your message appropriately. For example, if you are talking to a business reporter for your local paper you will want to pitch your business in a different way than if you are taking to a potential customer or an investor.

6. Reciprocate. Give the person you are talking to the opportunity to give their own elevator speech.

ciations include the American Mushroom Institute, the American Pie Council, the National Association of Convenience Stores, the Hosiery Association, the U.S. Poultry & Egg Association, and Printing Industries of America. In other words, if you are in a particular industry or business, there is quite probably a corresponding association. Also note that there are many state-specific trade associations (the Pennsylvania Newspaper Association, for example).

Trade associations[6] can serve as useful resources, not just in the preparatory stages of setting up your business (they can sometimes help answer industry-specific questions and provide news and information about pertinent law and regulatory changes), but also as promotional outlets. Many associations have meetings—either large national or international conferences and conventions, or smaller state and regional events—which can provide educational and networking—or public speaking—opportunities. Association publications, either online or in print, can also offer potential venues for you to communicate your expertise to others in your industry.

You can find organizations or associations in your line of work by Googling, say, "management consulting association" and finding, at the top of the hits, the Association of Management Consulting Firms (AMCF). Add your state or even city to your Google search to find any local chapters or local events. Also check your local newspaper, especially if your region has a business publication, for upcoming events.

AMERICAN MARKETING ASSOCIATION

The American Marketing Association (AMA[7]) is a national organization that keeps marketing professionals up to date on the latest trends in marketing communications. The AMA has local chapters around the country which offer guest speakers, networking events, and a variety of print and online publications. Find a chapter at www.marketingpower.com.

---

[6] A thorough but nowhere near complete list can be found at http://bit.ly/1mNgtFr.
[7] Not to be confused with the American Medical Association.

SERVICE ORGANIZATIONS

Many small business owners join local chapters of international or national service organizations, such as the Rotary International (www.rotary.org), Kiwanis (sites.kiwanis.org), Lions Clubs International (www.lionsclubs.org), and others. These groups usual-ly meet weekly, often for lunch, and are designed not only to be business net-

working events, but they also serve the community in some fashion, such as organizing benefits and fundraisers for various causes, staging events like home shows and fitness expos, and much more. Some require more of a time commitment than others, but all can be good opportunities for you both professionally—and personally.

TOASTMASTERS

Toastmasters International is an organization dedicated to helping its members develop and improve their communication and leadership skills. Toastmasters clubs help members get over the fear of public speaking (the number one reason people join Toastmasters) and helps them become better speakers and all-around communicators. Toastmasters has a lot to offer its members, especially small or independent businesspeople. Club meetings, regional contests and conferences,

and other events provide ample networking opportunities, and very often Toastmasters looking for products or services will seek out other Toastmasters. Meetings are great venues in which to rehearse professional presentations and get valuable feedback, as well as give speeches that promote your business—and hone your elevator speech. Find a club near you at www.toastmasters.org.

Unless you live in a very remote region, the chances are good that there are in-person networking events near you. If you are not adept at networking, the key—at least to start—is to not overextend yourself. You may think that "more is more" when it comes to these kinds of events, but it's best to pick perhaps two or at most three networking events over the course of a month, just to get a feel for them. If you find that you are having success with these events, by all means attend more, but you don't want to reach the point where networking and searching for new clients is taking time away from actual productive work for present clients.

Follow-Up

Regardless of which and how many networking events you attend, the most important part is the follow-up. Think about how many people you meet at an event, and assume that the people you met also met as many if not more. So how likely is it that you'll be remembered, or that you'll remember someone you have met. It's not uncommon to revisit a set of business cards collected at an event even two days later and not remember who someone was. So, it's a good idea to jot some kind of reminder on the business card itself, be it some distinctive aspect of the conversation ("said he liked to play jazz piano") or even his or her appearance ("looked like guy from *Walking Dead*"). Essentially, make note of anything that will trigger your memory of what you talked about.

Opinions vary as to how long you should wait before you follow up with someone you met an event, but generally one to five days is recommended. It doesn't have to be anything formal, just a quick e-mail saying "Enjoyed meeting you last night" and reminding him or her that you are interested in pursuing what you talked about. If during the event the prospect of meeting again one-on-one was mentioned, add "I'd love to sit down and talk with you in more detail about _____ when your schedule permits." You want to be tactful; a wrong approach to follow-up would be to write a note while in your car right after the event and say "Let's meet tomorrow at 12:30 and sign a contract!" It's like dating; there is a difference between "expressing interest" and being a "creepy stalker type." Or at least there should be.

There is also the very real possibility that the other person will be the one to follow up first.

Another integral part of follow-up is after acquiring someone's business card, to immediately send them a LinkedIn link request (see Chapter 6 about LinkedIn).

Moving Forward

Technology has made it easier than ever to stay in contact with colleagues. clients, and managers. Whether it is casual communication like instant messaging or Skype, or elaborate "virtual meetings," you can accomplish most of these things from the comfort of your home office. Just keep mentally repeating the mantra: convey a professional appearance at all times.

That said, there are also times when you will need—if not want—to get out of the office and network. After all, this is often how we get new business. And speaking of how we get new business, we'll look at marketing and promotion in the next chapter.

To Do:

❑ Identify the means by which you will need to stay in contact with colleagues, coworkers, or clients. AIM? Skype? iChat? A proprietary corporate messaging system?

❑ Experiment with the software and know how to tell potential messagers that you are receptive—or not—to communicating.

❑ You may not need to set up tele- or video-conferences immediately, but if you anticipate needing to, explore some of the options covered in this chapter well beforehand.

❑ Write and craft your elevator speech. Practice it on friends, family, or colleagues. Revise, revise, revise, and practice, practice, practice.

❑ Identify two or three in-person networking events over the course of the next month and develop some realistic expectations of what you want to get out of the event. Then, of course, go to them.

CHAPTER

Give Yourself a Promotion

"Business has only two basic functions—marketing and innovation."
—Peter Drucker, business theorist and author

"Nothing in the world can replace persistence."
—Calvin Coolidge, 30th President of the United States

Answer These Questions:

Do you have the basic marketing "collateral" materials: business cards, letterhead, envelopes?

Do you have a Web site?

How do you plan to promote or market your business and the services you offer?

Do you know best media "channels" to use to reach potential clients?

How active are you on social media?

How much time a week do you plan—or are willing—to dedicate to strictly marketing and promotional activities?

In the last chapter, we discussed networking and how networking events can be used for promoting your business and finding new customers. There are many other ways of achieving these objectives. We also talked about the "elevator speech," which can serve as an important foundation for all your other promotions. Rehearsing, revising, and tweaking the pitch gives you immediate feedback. Once it's refined, it can be used as a theme for your website, newsletter, social media, and all the other things we will be discussing in this chapter.

In this chapter, we will discuss many of the physical and technological means of promoting ourselves, but what we will be concentrating on is marketing and promotion as a *process*. Regardless of the media you choose for promotion, the key elements are diligence and persistence. We can only attract clients and customers by...well, by attracting them. You don't get clients if no one knows you exist!

Promotion, like the business itself, requires persistence and perseverance. We may not *want* to do it, but we have to.

There is no shortage of "channels"[1] for marketing and promoting a business these days, and the trick is to pick the channel or combination of channels through which you are most likely to reach your intended audience. In other words, where do you find the

> ### Shameless Self-Promotion
>
> Some people are very good at self-promotion, and others are much shyer about it. The comfort level likely goes back to our innate extrovert vs. introvert tendencies. Regardless, if we intend to be successful in our home business, we need to overcome whatever hesitancy we have toward self-promotion and "just do it" (to coin a phrase).

people most likely to be your customers? Are they on the whole not technologically proficient, never check e-mail, and have no idea what Facebook is? Or are they highly tech-savvy, find e-mail to be too slow

---

[1] By "channels" we mean the specific media through which we communicate a promotional message about our businesses. A TV ad is one channel, a newspaper ad is another. A Facebook page is another channel, as is a Twitter feed. Although we often lump all of "social media" together as a single chapter, each has its own nuances.

and archaic, and would never think of picking up the phone?[2] If the former, you may still need to resort to offline channels like print and television, and if the latter, you will have to become as tech-savvy as they are.

Marketing and Business Collateral

Before you do anything, though, you will need what is known as marketing "collateral." It's a fancy term, but all it refers to is the basic logistical and practical materials that support your business: business cards, letterhead, envelopes, and mailing labels. Oh, and there is one more thing: a website.

Let's look at these briefly in turn.

BUSINESS CARDS

Even in today's almost entirely electronic world, you still need good old-fashioned printed business cards. There are few, if any, satisfactory electronic alternatives, especially if you are out physically networking with people.[3] If you are a teleworker for a parent company, you will likely have business cards provided for you, and while they will have your phone number and e-mail address, all other information will likely be that of the company's headquarters. That may or

VistaPrint offers inexpensive business cards, even two-color (reproduced here in black-and-white) and two-sided, the latter a good way to avoid cluttering up a single side.

---

[2] It's tempting to assume these things are a function of age, but there are many young people who have no interest in social media or smartphones, and many older people—even seniors—who are highly technologically savvy.
[3] Back in the 1990s, when the Palm Pilot and related personal digital assistants (PDAs) came out, they had the ability to "beam" contact info from one device to another. That never really caught on, and the PDA itself has been replaced by smartphones. There are apps that will let you transfer information (contacts as well as just about anything else) from one device to another—the Chirp app (chirp.io) is one—but like its forebear, has yet to catch on.

L'eggo My Logo

Once you have decided on your business name, you may also decide that you want a logo. A logo can be as simple as the name of your business in a distinctive or unique typeface and color. Either you (or a graphic designer) can design a distinctive logo that embodies, in one icon, your business, like the Nike "swoosh" or McDonald's Golden Arches. You don't have to be that ambitious; in the short term, you should focus on building your business and not overthinking a logo. If, at some time in the future, you do come up with a great or better logo, you can switch to it and call it a "rebranding."

If you do want to develop a logo, some things to consider:

1. Make sure it's appropriate to your business. If you are operating a funeral home, you would not want a dancing Grim Reaper to be your logo. Professional services such as attorneys, accountants, financial planners, and medical professionals typically use very staid, conservative type and logos, as they're trying to convey professionalism and seriousness. On the other hand, if you are a professional party clown, you will likely want to go in the opposite direction.

2. If your own name is all or part of the business name, your stylized initial or initials can serve as a simple but effective logo.

3. Images that reflect your business type can make for good logos. If you are a dogwalker, use a dog on a leash; if you are a haircutter, an elaborate hairdo or scissors; if you are a personal trainer, a set of weights; if you are a data analyst, some kind of graph or chart.

4. Choose a specific color and make sure you always use that exact color. Color is very much a component of what we call "branding" and is an integral part of the logo.

5. Do a Google search for other businesses in the same field as yours and check out their web pages. What logos do they use? How effective or appealing do you, as a stranger visiting their business for the first time, find them?

6. Do a generic Google Images search for "company logos." You'll get a ton of hits and some may trigger some inspiration.

If you have the budget, you can also hire a graphic designer to develop a logo for you, but for someone just starting out in a home business, that may be overkill.

may not be a bad thing; it all depends on whether or not if you need to provide your direct mailing address to others.

What should appear on your business card? Some things are obvious, some things not.

- Your name and a title, if you have one, such as "President,"[4] "Principal," "Owner," and so on. If you are the only employee, it is acceptable to not include a title, but adding one does look a bit more professional.

- Company name and logo (if you have one—see sidebar).

- Mailing address. This is the address you decided to use for all business mail (see Chapter 3).

- Phone number(s). Again, this is the number—landline and/ or cell—you decided to use for business calls.

- E-mail address. Ditto.

- Website (see below).

- Brief bulleted list of the services you provide, even if you think it's obvious from the name of the company. For example, your business name may indicate that you are an attorney. What kind of attorney? Real estate? Copyright? Criminal? A business card functions as an ad, so use it as such.

- Some people also put their various social media (Facebook, Twitter, LinkedIn) addresses on their business cards, but that tends to make the card look too densely packed. When you set up your website (see below), you will have links to your other Internet presences, so it's not necessary to include them all on one card.

We've seen some people put QR (Quick Response, see later in this chapter) codes on their business cards—usually on the back— which will theoretically allow people with smartphones to scan the

---

[4] Avoid giving yourself a cutesy title like "Chief Cook and Bottle Washer." This trend was briefly popular (and thankfully short-lived) in the 1990s.

code and immediately access your website or whatever destination you program into the code. In reality, however, the number of times we have seen someone actually scan a QR code on a business card is zero to none. At this stage, all a QR code communicates is, "I know what a QR code is." Not that QR codes aren't important on other printed materials, but on business cards they are just taking up space that could be better utilized.

Business cards are fairly easy to either buy or create yourself. If you like a DIY approach, you can design your own and print them on perforated business card sheets sold at any office superstore. These sheets can be run through any laser or inkjet printer, and the quality is generally acceptable. This is a good option if you need a small batch of cards immediately, but they can be a little cheesy compared to professionally produced and printed cards unless you have a high-quality office printer.

You can also order business cards in bulk from many commercial printers. Vistaprint (www.vistaprint.com) has become a reliable source for business cards and other print and non-print services. The company has focused on small businesses, especially home offices, and it offers free business cards, only charging for shipping. Of course, you are limited to their own designs (some of which are better than others), and you can't add your own logo, but they're free. You can also pay to have additional layers of customization.

Letterhead, Envelopes, and Mailing Labels

You may or may not have an immediate need for these items, but as with business cards you can opt for the do-it-yourself approach (store a template on your computer in Microsoft Word, Adobe InDesign, or the application of your choice) and then print them out as needed. You can buy blank letterhead paper at an office superstore. Most laser and inkjet printers today can print on envelopes, and you can buy sheets of labels that can also be run through a printer. If you only physically mail things once in a blue moon, this is a cost-effective option.

If you do plan to be mailing frequently, you may be able to get a package deal on all these materials with the commercial printing company that prints your business cards.

THE WEBSITE: THE NEW BUSINESS CARD

In the last chapter, we talked about attending networking events, and earlier in this chapter, we discussed business cards. Would you think of attending a networking event without bringing business cards? How would anyone ever get in touch with you afterward? Sure, you can rattle off your e-mail address and/or phone number and hope they'll remember them, but that really isn't likely. And while you could also write your contact info on a cocktail napkin, that is rather unprofessional. So, yes, business cards are a business must-have.

But there is something that, over the course of the past twenty years, has become just as important—if not more so—than the business card. And that is a web site.

In 2012, we published *"Does a Plumber Need a Web Site?"*,[5] a title that was inspired by an attendee at one of Dr. Joe's presentations. And the answer is absolutely yes. A plumber—or *any* business—needs to have a website. A good business website lists the services or products that your business offers, provides examples (such as writing or design samples), offers testimonials from customers, has e-commerce capabilities (if applicable), and above all offers ways to contact you.[6]

The specific steps involved in setting up a website are beyond the scope of this book—entire books could be (and have been) written about that topic—but we'll offer some tips to get you started off in the right direction.

---

[5] Check it out at http://bit.ly/1sK9AHC.
[6] Some companies are simply using their Facebook business page as their official website. While this approach is free and adequate, we strongly recommend setting up your own unique, professional-looking web site.

Buying vs. Registering Domain Names

There is a difference between *buying* and merely *registering* a domain name. You would only buy a domain—which can range from a few hundred to a few thousand dollars—if you wanted one that someone else had already registered and was selling. If you sold pet supplies and really wanted pets.com, you could pay big bucks to PetSmart (the current owner of that domain), although it's doubtful they would relinquish it. Less in-demand domains may also be already taken. If you wanted to use your name as your domain, and someone having the same name as you already had reserved that domain, you may be able to buy the domain name from them, if they weren't using it. Adding your middle name or initial may be one way around this.

Some domains are bought by brokers and "parked." This means that someone has bought a domain—usually one that has a combination of English words that someone someday may want to use, like, say, DigitalInspiration—and is hanging onto it until they find a buyer. Then they negotiate a price for it. And speaking of website addresses, make sure that you get something that users won't find confusing. "DigitalInspiration" has a lowercase "L" and an uppercase "I" in the middle, which can be confusing when written or in text. One blog site about writing, "Pen Is Mightier," found that its web address "penismightier.com" was, um, easily misread.

If your desired domain name is *not* being used by anyone else, all you need to do is register it—which is pretty inexpensive (less than $50 for two years). websites that end in .us, .info, .biz, or others, can be less expensive than .com addresses but are harder for others to remember since they are more used to seeing the familiar ".com." A quick way to see if your desired domain is available is to simply enter it in your web browser and see what comes up.

By the way, if you choose to use Gmail for your e-mail, you can have Google register a domain for you, which you can then use as your e-mail and web address. The cost starts at about $8 a month.

There are three overall steps involved in setting up a website:

- buying or registering a domain
- contracting with a web hosting company
- designing and producing the site's pages

Let's look a these issues in turn.

Branded.me and LinkedIn for Web Pages

We mentioned LinkedIn in the previous chapter, and we'll revisit it later in this one, but it's worth mentioning here that using the personal "branding platform" branded.me with LinkedIn might be the most efficient and inexpensive way

of getting a professional web page. Really finesse your LinkedIn page, make it a point to collect recommendations from colleagues and clients, and that can serve as the basis of your website. The LinkedIn template can then guide you better than many other web page-building alternatives.

You can then use it as your "official" web page, and because it's a business site and not something like Facebook, you gain credibility. Start at https://branded. me and click the Sign In With LinkedIn button.

Also be sure to take advantage of LinkedIn's close integration with the site Slideshare, which lets you post short presentations and videos that are easy to link to your LinkedIn page. This is a much-underutilized promotional platform.

Mastering Your Domain

Before you begin the process of setting up a website, you will want to register a "domain." A domain is your web address, technically called a URL, which stands for "Universal Resource Locator." If your Web address is www.mycompany.com, your domain is "mycompany.com." You can come up with any domain that is appropriate (with some cautions, which we'll cover in a minute), but if you want web browsers to be able to access it on the Web, you will need to register it with a web registrar, such as Register. com or GoDaddy.com[7]. Vistaprint offers this service now, so you can get business cards and register your website in one place.

When you visit a registrar, the first thing you will need to do is see if your desired domain is available. On the home screens of

---

[7] If you also need web hosting services—to be covered shortly—a chosen web host can also register your domain simultaneously, saving time and even a little money.

most registrars is typically a field wherein you can enter your desired website address, and it will tell you if it is available. If it isn't, you can try to negotiate with the owner for it (see sidebar), or—the better option—you can come up with another choice.[8]

One of the most important tips for picking a domain is to keep it short. It will not only be your web address but your e-mail address as well, and very often you have to spell out your e-mail address for people. The longer and more unwieldy it is, the more likely it is that people will get it wrong—or will get annoyed. Avoid using initials unless they are your business name. Get as close to the name of yourself or your business as possible—unless you have a very long business name.

Web Hosting

Once you have your domain, you will need to find a web host. This is simply a service provider that has the computer on which the files that comprise your website will physically be located.

Once you contract with a web host, you can start uploading the actual files that will comprise your site.

Website Design and Development

As with the other types of collateral we have discussed, you have several options for getting a website designed and developed. If you are technically proficient, you can do it yourself, and there are many tools today that do make it easy. Alternatively—and this is what we would recommend—hire a web designer. It's not that web design is difficult *per se*, but even if you have a decent background in print design and production, web design is not entirely user-friendly. It's one of those situations where if you don't know what you're doing, you can end up creating a website that hurts your business more than it helps. You'll also need to stay current on the latest web design technologies and best practices, lest you discover five or six years down the road that

---

[8] When you do an availability search for your domain, don't be discouraged if "mydomain.com" is taken. Dot-com is not the only option available. You may find that "mydomain.net," "mydomain.biz," etc., may be available, although there is something of a nagative connotation to a non-"com" URL—almost like the area code issue we discuss in the footnote on page 62.

Choosing A Web Host

What makes for a good or bad web hosting company? A good web host will:

- Have no (or absolutely minimal) server downtime. Server downtime means that no one can access your website—and you will not have access to e-mail—while that server is down. No web traffic means no business.

- Have 24/7 tech support in case there is a problem. Some have chat- or instant messaging-based customer support.

There are other issues as well, depending on your specific web needs, but for most basic web presences, these are the big two.

As with other technological matters, finding a web host is like finding other service providers: it's always best to get word-of-mouth recommendations.

A Google search will turn up no shortage of hosts, but who knows how reliable they will be? A good place to start is a directory of businesses that are members of your local Chamber of Commerce. If you are working with a web designer for the actual site, he or she likely knows of some hosts they or their other clients have worked with before.

A good start can often be to get your domain name through a hosting company, such as 1and1.com. They often offer domain registration discounts for buying a hosting package, and the packages often include e-mail accounts.

your website looks "ancient." Not all of us have the time to keep up with that aspect of technology.

Regardless of which route you take, here are some crucial elements that should be included in any website.

Every website has, by default, a home page. This is the first thing visitors see when they enter your web address in a browser. As a result, it should make the best first impression of your business. It should be attractively designed and meticulously proofread. It should explain succinctly what your business does and what products or services you offer. A written version of your elevator speech (see Chapter 5) would not be out of place either on your home page, or on an "About" page (see below).

Your home page should also include:

- Your logo or the customized type you use on your business card.

- Navigation buttons or other tools that clearly indicate how to get to other pages in your site, such as samples of your work (if it is something that can be shown on a website), testimonials from customers, a blog (if you have one), videos (if you have any), a detailed contact page, links to things you may have written that are on other websites, articles about you, and other promotional material.

- Contact information. Although you will want to have a detailed contact page that has your physical mailing address and any and all other contact info you care to provide, at the very least, your phone number and a hot link to your e-mail address should appear prominently on the home page—and, in fact, on every page of your website.

- "Chiclets." These are those little square icons that link to your Facebook, LinkedIn, Twitter, YouTube, or other social media sites (if you have them, and you should, see later in this chapter).

Time and a Word

There are benefits to using Wordpress as your website platform. Wordpress began as strictly blogging software, but it has evolved so that with only minimal amounts of programming, it can look less like a traditional blog and more like a "real" website. The big advantage is that, for the non-technical user, making changes is as easy as updating a blog, which means that you don't have to run all changes, however minor, through a web designer. Dr. Joe's official site at drjoewebb.com, developed by Interlink ONE using Wordpress, looks professional, and is easy to update.

Still, not everyone is happy with the Wordpress approach, but an alternative to is a web building tool called Wix (www.wix.com). It is free and offers thousands of customizable templates.

Whatever other pages you choose add to your site will be a function of the business you are in and whatever supplementary material you have to provide. A blog is a good addition to a web-

 Home About Dr. Joe Webb Blogs Additional Resources Contact Dr. Joe ENewsletter Sign Up

CONNECT WITH DR. JOE WEBB

THE OFFICIAL SITE OF DR. JOE WEBB
Consultant, Analyst, Forecaster

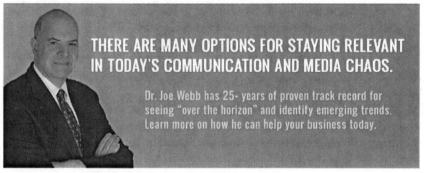

THERE ARE MANY OPTIONS FOR STAYING RELEVANT IN TODAY'S COMMUNICATION AND MEDIA CHAOS.

Dr. Joe Webb has 25+ years of proven track record for seeing "over the horizon" and identify emerging trends. Learn more on how he can help your business today.

Dr. Joe's home page (drjoewebb.com) succinctly identifies what he does (even though he's occasionally confused), and features clear site navigation and contact links.

site, as it gives you the opportunity to demonstrate the extent to which you are a credible expert in your chosen profession. You may hold regular events or classes and thus may want to add a calendar to your site and allow people register online. If you make and sell physical products, you may want to set up an e-commerce section on your website. You will need to talk with your web designer and/or web host about these types of options.

The basic function of your website is threefold:

- to explain who you are and what you do
- to showcase your work, or at least demonstrate why someone would hire you
- to ensure that your company will be found by a Google search

Think of a website as a promotional brochure, which is exactly what it is.

Sailing the Seas of SEO

A close look at "search engine optimization (SEO)" is beyond the scope of this book, but it is a means of ensuring that website content contains specific "keywords" that someone would search for so that your site would turn up toward the top of the first page of hits of a Google search. SEO also embeds keywords in the page code itself. There is an art and a science to SEO, and web consultants get paid a lot to optimize sites. You may not have the resources to go all out with SEO, but think about what word(s) a potential customer would enter in Google to find you. Make sure those keywords are included in the copy on your home page—but organically, not listed as an obvious set of keywords.

There are other marketing collateral materials you may want to produce. Printed brochures can be distributed at events or left in hotel lobbies, visitor centers, and other public "drop spots," depending on your business. And you should include downloadable PDF versions of these brochures and other printed materials on your website.

Responsive Design

A term you sometimes come across is "responsive design," or "responsive web design (RWD)," which refers to a website created in such a way that it will automatically detect what device is accessing it—laptop, tablet, or smartphone—and optimize the display accordingly. Responsive design may be important in and of itself, but most importantly, Google is changing its search algorithms so that responsively designed sites are ranked higher than regular sites." Since Google search is one of primary ways that businesses get found, this may be a very big deal to you. It might be worth having a conversation with a web designer or Internet consultant.

Developing a Marketing Strategy

Having a set of printed and electronic collateral materials is important, but so, too, is developing some kind of overall marketing and promotion strategy for your business. The channels that comprise that strategy will be a function of:

- your budget

- the time you have available for promotional activities ("none" is not an acceptable answer)

- the audience you are trying to reach

As a small business, you don't have to implement a campaign which is as costly and expansive as Pepsi, Nike, or some other large consumer corporation. And, in fact, you may not want your marketing to be *too* successful, otherwise you run into the problem of not being able to meet demand. That's a pleasant problem to have, but it's still a problem.

But we're getting ahead of ourselves.

Let's take a quick look at how things have changed over the last forty years or so.

The Way We Were: The 1970s

Small businesses in the 1970s and even the 1980s most often used some combination of the following media channels—depending on size and budget—to promote themselves[9]:

- word of mouth/referrals

- location/attractive signage, if allowed (see Chapter 1)

- Yellow Pages advertising

- display advertising in local newspaper

- TV ad on local station

- radio ad

- cold-calling prospects by phone or in person

- sponsoring local events, Little League teams, etc.

- printed brochures and other collateral materials (like business cards)

- custom printed proposals for each client

---

[9] Given the technology then, a home-based business was less feasible as it is today, so here we're speaking about small businesses generally, not necessarily home businesses.

- diner placemats
- vehicle graphics (hand-stenciled graphics or adhesive letters)
- trade show and other event attendance
- printed press releases to industry or local media

THE WAY WE ARE: THE 2010S

Here are the available channels for small businesses today, grouped into general categories:

Online

- website
- Google search
- paid search
- banner ad on high-traffic website
- Craigslist
- Superpages online entry
- e-mailed press releases to industry or local media
- direct e-mail
- e-newsletters

Print

- some advertising in local newspaper
- Yellow Pages listing
- business cards and other collateral
- specialty print (T-shirts, bumper stickers, magnets, pens, etc.)
- QR codes
- direct mail

Social Media

- Facebook pages/Facebook Groups
- Twitter
- LinkedIn profile/LinkedIn Groups
- blog
- online video (YouTube or on your own site)

Location Services[10]

- sites/apps like Yelp!
- Augmented Reality (AR)
- Groupon/Living Social

Offline

- word-of-mouth
- physical location/attractive signage
- radio advertising (terrestrial or satellite)
- local TV/cable advertising
- sponsoring community events
- speaking at workshops, seminars, briefings, trade shows, Chamber of Commerce events, and other public venues

Never heard of some of these items? Don't worry. You're not alone, and we'll examine them in turn. What's really scary is that this list is in no way complete!

Notice how some things have not changed...or have they? Word-of-mouth referrals, for example, are still highly effective for cultivating new business. What has changed is that "word-of-mouth" is now more often than not "word-of-*mouse*," in which there is some overlap with social media.

---

[10] By "location" services, we are referring to specific services that are typically accessed via a smartphone app, which is why "physical location" is not included in this category.

It's tempting to say, broadly, that offline channels (print, TV, radio) have been replaced by online channels (Web site, social media, search), but that is not entirely true. Let's look at some of these more closely.

Online Channels

A well-designed, easy-to-navigate **website** is vital for any twenty-first-century business. A well-optimized website is found when potential customers do **Google search**es. You can also take advantage of **paid search**, where you can pay Google to have your listing come up when certain keywords are searched.

You can also take out a **banner ad** on a high-traffic website, although it doesn't necessarily have to be high-traffic. It could be your local newspaper's website, a prominent blog in your industry, a local non-profit community or arts organization's site, and so on.

If you're old enough, you may remember newspaper classified advertising. **Craigslist** is sort of a modern equivalent of classified ads with the Yellow Pages thrown in, and all sorts of products and services are advertised and purchased via a Craigslist listing. It is entirely free, and each general geographic region has its own set of listings. Check it out at www.craigslist.com.

You may remember the Yellow Pages—the phone book, essentially—which has fallen into disrepute these days, although it still has its fans. **Superpages** is the Yellow Pages' online directory of businesses, and you can either get a free basic listing, or you can pay for display ads that appear on the Superpages site or on other websites. There is also a Yellow Pages smartphone app.

When you open your doors for business, complete major projects, land major accounts, win awards, or accomplish some other achievement, **e-mailed press releases to industry or local media** can help get the word out about it and can even lead to features in local newspapers or your local business press. Trade publications in your industry are also always looking for news to "feed the beast" of daily online publishing.

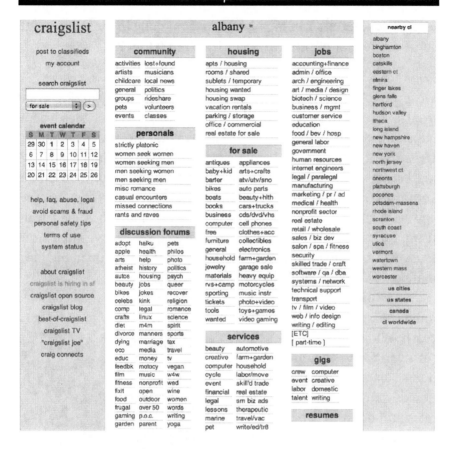

Direct e-mail, as you probably know intimately from being on the receiving end of it, is a promotional e-mail message sent to a mailing list of current or potential customers to promote a product, service, or upcoming event. Some e-mail campaigns blur the line between direct e-mail and electronic newsletters (see below). Some blur the line between legitimate campaigns and spam.

An **e-newsletter** is an e-mail-distributed publication that provides news, information, and commentary related to the industry your business is in. The primary difference between an e-newsletter and direct e-mail is that a newsletter should be news- and information-based, rather than strictly promotional. The frequency of e-newsletters can be anywhere from daily to monthly—with some outliers publishing more or less frequently.

Print

We probably don't need to spend a lot of time explaining what print is (we hope!). Although a lot has been made of the decline in print newspaper circulation, in many communities local papers still serve a vital purpose, and advertising in them remains a viable marketing strategy. So depending on the status of your local paper, **some advertising in local newspaper** may be a worthwhile strategy (you may also get a package rate that includes banner advertising on the paper's website). Also don't discount weekly "Moneysavers" and those other free publications that turn up in people's mailboxes. They are still very effective.

A **Yellow Pages listing** may not be as important these days as online search, but again, it is a function of whom you are trying to reach. While people under thirty (or even forty) may not use the phone book to find local businesses anymore, many older folks still do, so if you are targeting them, you may want to include a display ad in the phone book as part of your marketing strategy.

We spoke about **business cards and other collateral** earlier in this chapter, but don't ignore assorted specialty print **(T-shirts, bumper stickers, refrigerator magnets, pens, posters, etc.)**.

Specialty products like T-shirts can be great promotional items and don't have to cost a fortune. Many are appropriate to a given business. They also make great gifts for longtime and loyal customers.

These items may not be as expensive as you think, and everyone still needs them. If you are going to attend or exhibit at a trade event, novelties can get your name in front of potential customers. The key to these specialty items is to make them useful. A pen is useful. A refrigerator magnet is useful. But a pin-back button? It may look nice, but really, who is ever going to wear it any-where? Decide what might actually come in handy and what will likely end up thrown in a junk drawer.

When we discussed **QR codes** in the con-text of printing them on business cards, we were a bit dismissive. But there is a place for QR codes in even a small business' marketing plan. And they cost nothing. A Quick Response (QR) code is a type of bar code that, when scanned with a smartphone camera and QR reader app,

In Our Experience: QR Training

Richard was once in a Chicago subway station, and on a pillar across the tracks was a poster that had a QR code on it. However, the only way you could get close enough to scan the code would be to climb down on the tracks.

On another note, if you use a QR code, make sure it links to a permanent page or site—and keep ensuring that it's up to date.

launches a website, video, or some other type of interactive or immersive experience. They are best employed on posters and flyers—outdoor real estate advertising, for example. You pass a new set of condos, and there is a sign with a QR code that, when scanned, launches pictures of the in-terior, the floor plan, and other rental or purchase information. Although the QR code is perhaps best thought of as a transitional technology (better ways of accomplishing the same thing already exist), it's a good way of driv-ing people to a website in places where it is not convenient for them to laboriously type a URL.

And let's not forget old-fashioned **direct mail**. Postcards, bro-chures, one-page flyers, etc., can be printed and mailed to a prospect list. Direct mail is more expensive than direct e-mail or other elec-tronic communications, but it can be more effective. Not everyone is a fan of so-called "junk mail," but in this day and age where we get so little physical mail anymore, it can actually be the best way to attract someone's attention. An e-mail can and will, in all likelihood, be deleted sight unseen in the average user's morning mailbox purge of overnight messages. Direct mail can be static (you send the same thing to everyone) or variable (you customize or personalize each piece in some way so that it is more likely to be relevant to the recipient), and a detailed look at the distinctions is beyond the scope of this book. Printed variable direct mail does have better response rates than generic direct mail. The key to any direct mail campaign is that it must be relevant, and it works best when it includes some kind of offer, such as a discount or some other incentive.

Building Mailing Lists

How do you acquire the addresses of potential e-mail or e-newsletter recipients? You can certainly buy mailing lists from list brokers or from publications, although this route is not cheap. However, when you go to networking events (see Chapter 5) and collect business cards, this contact info can help build a mailing list. It's always preferable to ask, "Can I put you on my mailing list?" or "Would you like to receive my e-newsletter?" before you start sending anything. Your e-newsletters should also encourage the forwarding of the newsletter to others who might have similar interests. And always give recipients the ability to cancel their subscription. Sending unwanted e-mail can be the best way to drive away potential new business, and there are also laws about sending unsolicited marketing-based e-mail messages. Companies like Constant Contact have excellent ways of managing the process, and it has online instructional programs in the marketing of small businesses.

Social Media

Short for "Web log," the idea of the **blog** began back in the 1990s as a kind of online diary, where techies would detail the minutiae of their lives which, as you can imagine, was utterly compelling. Since then, blogs have evolved into a hybrid magazine article/editorial, and the best ones provide information, opinion, and perspective on some area of interest. For businesses, especially small businesses, blogs are excellent ways to demonstrate expertise and knowledge, provide advice, tips, strategies, etc.

Every Door Direct Mail (EDDM)

The U.S. Postal Service (USPS) is actually a much better business resource than we typically give it credit for—or even know about. The USPS offers a variety of services that businesses can utilize. Take, for example, Every Door Direct Mail (http://1.usa.gov/1hfnNDv), an online tool that lets you target print direct mail campaigns literally by street. If you only wanted to reach homes and businesses in a three-mile radius around your physical location, you could do it. There are four steps to using Every Door Direct Mail:

1. Register (natch).

2. Define your target area by ZIP code, city, or state. It will even let you specify specific streets and intersections.

3. Create your mailpiece. The website also offers a list of local printers who are conversant in the postal requirements for this system.

4. Pay and mail.

The online tool lets you select individual mail carrier routes, interactively tells you how many addresses are in each route, and specifies the cost for each route. This way you can keep within whatever budget you have set. Just selecting six carrier routes in ZIP code 12866, for example, translates to 3,273 addresses and would cost $523.68 (just for the postage, not the printing of the mail piece). Depending how well you know your local area, you may know that there is a brand new subdivision where the new residents might make good prospects. With this tool you can target those new homes. Be sure to poke around the Business Solutions pages on the USPS web site. There are a number of educational and training tools available.

With Every Door Direct Mail, you can select entire ZIP codes or individual carrier routes, and the interactive tool will automatically calculate the number of mailing addresses and the postage cost.

There are three primary blogging platforms: Blogger (owned by Google), TypePad, and WordPress. A basic blog is completely free and is easy to set up. Some of the blog providers have for-pay premium services (usually about $20 a year) that give you more control over the look and feel of the site graphics, as well as the ability to integrate the blog onto a parent website. (This is important if you want the URL of the blog to have your own domain and not wordpress.com or blogspot.com.) You can also have your website developer incorporate a blog into your own site, which can be a substantial cost. The downside to blogging is that it can require a substantial time commitment, depending on how easy or difficult you find writing. One option is to simply come up with the main points and farm out the actual writing to others, either for free (such as an intern or family member) or for pay.

Going Social

Social media has become one of the biggest forces in marketing and promotion today. It's typically referred to in the context of "joining the conversation." The misunderstanding that many people have with social media marketing is the expectation that it will generate X dollars of revenue or new business in Y period of time. This is the wrong way to think about it. Social media marketing—social networking—is best thought of as akin to in-person networking, as we discussed in the last chapter. It's about gaining visibility and building relationships that may eventually pay off over time. You don't go to a networking event with the expectation of landing five new customers right on the spot. So, too, should you not launch a social media marketing strategy and expect it to produce immediate results. It takes time—and, more importantly, it takes diligence and persistence.

Related to blogs are **podcasts**, which are audio recordings much like short radio programs or features that offer news, commentary, instruction, advice, interviews, or other content—the same sort of things you would out in a blog, except it is in audio format.[11]

The blog evolved (or devolved, perhaps) into what is called microblogging, or very short blog posts. Exemplified by **Twitter**, mi-

---

[11] The built-in A/V capabilities of today's computers and even mobile devices make it easier than ever to record and distribute a podcast. A detailed instruction is beyond the scope of this book, but a good place to start is here: http://bit.ly/1vwxmaS.

croblogging functions like a blog but posts can only be a maximum of 140 characters. That sounds like scarcely enough space in which to say anything particularly poignant, but you'd be surprised. Users who have a Twitter "feed" attract "followers" and in turn follow others. Twitter also fosters more or less real-time conversations, and "tweets" (as Twitter posts are called) can be "retweeted" by a particular user's followers, which can attract other followers. Any respectable person or event these days has an accompanying "hashtag" (#) which indicates that it is something that can be followed on Twitter. Like other social media channels, Twitter is free (which explains its popularity; if it were for-pay, it would be nowhere), but does require a more or less substantial time commitment not only to do the actual tweeting, but also to monitor others' feeds for mentions.

It is common practice and Twitter etiquette to follow those who have followed you. However, don't feel obligated to follow everyone; some tweeters just seek to maximize their followers, regardless of how relevant or receptive those followers may be. Try to limit the users you follow to only the most relevant to your business.

You have no doubt by now have at least heard of **Facebook**, a social networking site where users create

> ## Beat the Retweet
>
> Retweeting—sending a tweet from someone you follow to your own followers—can be good public relations, and if your own retweets get retweeted, it demonstrates a certain level of "influence." It can be a good marketing gambit.

profiles of themselves, add friends, post status updates, share photos and videos, etc.

For businesses, the most relevant aspect of Facebook is setting up a separate page for your company. That is, you create a profile, post status updates, and encourage others to become fans, often via links on other Web sites or blogs, or in your personal Facebook status feed. Once your friends "like" your business page, any news updates you post on that page will appear in their news feeds. This is a handy tool for keeping your social network informed of any awards, accomplishments, milestones, or events.

If you are planning an event—such as a workshop or some other appearance—you can also create an "event page" in Facebook that provides the logistic information on attending, and you can invite your Facebook friends as well as see who has accepted or declined your invitation.

Some Facebook Cautions

Some businesses use their Facebook page as their official business Web site, but, again, we would advise against this strategy. Facebook is totally free for its users, but that free-dom does (arguably) give Facebook the right to change its privacy policies at a moment's notice—which it does, and not for the benefit of users. But, hey, it's their house, and as long as you live under their roof, you'll do what they say. Not everyone is happy about this, and it's for this reason—among others—that a lot of people, even very tech-savvy people, refuse to join Facebook. And, in fact, we've seen some data suggest that Facebook is becoming unpopular among younger people, which does not bode well for its future viability. (And remember that at one time MySpace was the hot social media site, so nothing is forever.) Social media as a whole is certainly not a fad, but relying solely on any one particular site or implementation of social media is not a good long-term strategy. Our best advice with Facebook is to take advantage of it while it's hot, but be prepared to abandon it if and when everyone else does, and keep an eye out for the next social media destination.

Facebook also has Groups that you can join and then connect with other like-minded individuals. They are best thought of as clubs, the kind you would join in the offline world: go to meetings, participate in discussions, and meet and network with other members of the group. Facebook Groups function in much the same way; members discuss various topics more or less interactively. Facebook Groups aren't necessarily as useful for business as LinkedIn Groups (see below), but depending on the business you are in, can be good for building up a network of contacts and potential sales leads. As with anything in the social media sphere, it is best to avoid direct sales pitches or to seem like you are overtly trawling for business. The idea is to provide cogent, helpful, or informative comment and content.

As we mentioned earlier, Facebook was not originally designed as a tool for businesses, but they have since launched new tools and services to make the platform more suitable for business users. Most prominently, you can create Facebook ads—but we would advise against that. No one likes ads on social media, and you are much better off building Likes and reposts organically. Still, Facebook ads have worked for some. Start at https://www.facebook.com/business and explore your options.

LinkedIn is much like Facebook, but it is a better approach to social media for business.[12] Users on LinkedIn are there specifically for professional networking, which keeps the level of conversation higher than on Facebook (which isn't hard). There are several components to using LinkedIn effectively for business:

- *Profile.* It's worth devoting extra time to working on your Linke-dIn profile, as this is the "ad" that will attract contacts. Describe what products or services you offer clearly and concisely, but

avoid sounding like an ad. Pay special attention to a profile picture; *do not* attempt a self-portrait with a cameraphone (aka "selfie") as they never look good. You may even want to spend a little money and have a professional photo taken. This can be used on LinkedIn as well as on your own Web site and for any other promotional

purposes. Remember, the key word in everything you put out to promote your business should be "professional."

- *Contacts.* Naturally, you will want to add contacts, otherwise no one will see your profile. How do you get started? Begin with people you personally know; search for them on LinkedIn, and if they have a profile, send a request to connect.[13] Once you start

[12] It is also our opinion that LinkedIn will have greater longevity than Facebook, although like anything online will not be popular forever.
[13] You can't just willy-nilly add people to your contact list; you have to send them an

amassing contacts, LinkedIn will often suggest mutual contacts, and at the same you will start receiving connect requests. It's tempting to add everyone who wants to connect, but as with Facebook and Twitter, you are searching for quality not quantity. If someone very far afield of your business sends a connect request, give some thought to whether you want to accept.

In Our Experience: Linking In

Dr. Joe really enjoys the weekly LinkedIn podcast "The Missing Link" (http:// rainmaker.fm/series/link/). Rainmaker.fm has a lot of other podcasts that are appropriate for home offices. LinkedIn also now owns Slideshare—where you can post slide decks from presentations—and the two services are very well integrated. One way of taking advantage of this is by turning blogposts into Slideshare shows or minipresentations. We are ourselves in the process of working on this.

Your elevator speech (remember the last chapter?) can also serve as the basis for a short minipresentation that can be posted on Slideshare.

- *LinkedIn Premium.* The free "default" LinkedIn services limits the members whom you can contact. That is, you can only send messages to those to whom you are directly linked. But maybe you want to reach out to those beyond your immediate circle. LinkedIn has a variety of premium tiers (which start at $29.95 a month) that vary based on whether you are a job hjunter, a job seeker, a business seekling to grow your network, or are looking specifically for sales leads. A premium account let you send "InMail" to anyone on LinkedIn, and also give you more access even to those already in your circle. It's worth reviewing the options at https://premium.linkedin.com.

- *Status Updates.* Here you can post any news about your business, such as projects you have completed, awards you have attained, new clients you have landed, personal appearances, and so forth. It is also helpful to share links to stories or other content you have

---

invitation and wait for them to accept (or not). Don't take it personally if someone doesn't accept your invitation; it may just mean they are not a big LinkedIn user.

come across online—related to your industry—and add a brief comment. Try to craft intelligent and helpful comments; this can be very good PR for yourself if you can demonstrate enough expertise in a subject to comment on it in an insightful way.

- *Groups.* As with Facebook, you can start and/or join LinkedIn Groups, a collection of LinkedIn members in the same industry or discussing a specific topic. This is a good way to share insights and other links and information. As always, remember to be professional.

- *Recommendations.* If you have worked with any of your contacts regularly or on major projects, ask them to write you a recommendation which can be added to your profile. Have them be specific. While it would be disingenuous for you to write a recommendation yourself and have them post it under their own name, it's not uncommon to go back and forth a few times via e-mail to ensure that your recommender is emphasizing the kind of work you want to get more of. And, of course, be sure to return the favor and write a recommendation for a recommender, if they desire one.

As with any social media initiative, it requires a certain amount of regular activity, diligence, and persistence to bear fruit. We may not *like* doing it, but it's become a necessary evil today, and will likely remain that way, however much we may think it's just a passing fad (it isn't). Come up with a schedule for devoting time to social media activities—say, from 3:00 to 4:00 P.M. This could also be tied into a set period of catching up on industry-related news; get into a habit of setting aside a time to read trade news, checking out links from our Twitter-mates, our Google news alerts, and other educational activities. While doing this, share interesting links and offer comment on them. Once this becomes a regular habit, it will become easier and more natural, and at the same time you'll be increasing your presence among your social network. Relinks, retweets, and other "forwards" can help expand your network.[14]

There are a tremendous number of ways of taking advantage of LinkedIn. If you have read the Greatest Strengths report (see page 208) and taken the evaluation, your results can be linked to your LinkedIn page, so visitors can get a sense of what it's like to work with you.

There are many good LinkedIn resources. For example, Wayne Breitbarth has many free resources, including several ebooks.[15] Using his methods you can get the most out of LinkedIn using just the free service.

One last type of social media that should not be overlooked is **online video**, either on YouTube or on your own site. This may sound overly ambitious and complicated, but today's consumer videocameras[16] and related software have made it cheaper and easier than ever to record and post video. Some ideas for what to record and post:

- Commentary on topics of interest in your industry, *à la* a blog or podcast. If you are an accountant, perhaps you could provide a short discussion on changes in tax laws.

- Step-by-step instruction on some activity in your field of business. If you are a personal trainer, perhaps you can demonstrate a particular exercise. If you teach software training, you can show how to perform a task in a given application.

- A public presentation. If you are speaking in front of a group or at an event, take advantage of the opportunity by setting up your video camera (a tripod can be had for under $20 at Target) and recording and posting the presentation. You can also post audio only, if that is more convenient.

- An interview. Interview a colleague, or have a colleague interview you about a project you have worked on—or even on some current topic in your field of business.

- A clip of you giving your "elevator speech" (see page 94).

[14] If you really want to get the most out of LinkedIn, check out Wayne Breitbarth's book *The Power Formula for LinkedIn Success* at www.powerformula.net.
[15] See http://www.powerformula.net/free-resources-for-learning-linkedin.
[16] A decent quality videocamera sells for under $200 at BestBuy, Amazon, or elsewhere.

Videos should not be long (three to five minutes is ideal, although public presentations will be longer), and they can be divided into several installments if necessary. Videos can be posted on your own website, on your blog, and on any and all of your other social media sites. You can also start your own channel on YouTube. A YouTube video here (http://bit.ly/1FZRS6M) explains how to set up a YouTube channel.

There are other social media channels like **Pinterest** and **Instagram** that are gaining in popularity. Instagram (http://instagram.com) is a photo- and video-sharing site/smartphone app (recently acquired by Facebook) while Pinterest (https://pinterest.com) is a site—that integrates with Facebook—to share content that interests you in some way.

Location Services

"Location services" is a catchall term for several different types of mobile device apps that use the geographical location of the device to identify businesses nearby, typically grouped by category. For most home businesses, these kinds of apps are not entirely relevant, but we feel you should have a passing familiarity with at least some of them.

Yelp! is a website and complementary smartphone app that functions as a combination local directory and user review site. Not only does it let users find businesses by ZIP code or by using the location of the mobile device, it also lets users add reviews. Yelp! also lets users check in at locations, tell friends where they are, and add comments. Perhaps most helpful for finding restaurants, bars, drug stores, gas stations, and other such places when traveling, it can also function as the Yellow Pages once did. AroundMe is another app that works in a similar way.

Foursquare is a smartphone app that determines the user's geographic location and suggests nearby businesses. Users can upload reviews or tips concerning that business. Foursquare used to have a "check-in" feature, but spun that off into a separate app called Swarm. (Facebook has a similar feature.) Some businesses have run Foursquare-centric promotions, and the company offers various options for businesses. Truthfully, through, most individuals and businesses stick to Facebook these days, for better or worse.

Augmented Reality (AR) refers to any of a variety of ways of "overlaying" information—video, audio, graphics, etc.—over a physical location when viewed through a smartphone camera and an AR app. A very simple application of AR is the Yelp! app's Monocle feature that shows you what is nearby.

Groupon/Living Social are "deal-of-the-day" websites—Amazon Local is Amazon's own approach to deal-of-the-day marleting—that features discounted gift certificates usable at local or national companies

Mobile phone apps like Yelp! let users find businesses near them. Such mobile apps are quickly replacing Yellow Pages and even Google. You can offer products or services on user "check-ins," which can then be searched.

Yelp!'s Monocle feature, a primitive form of AR, overlays nearby businesses on the phone viewscreen.

in a wide variety of business categories. The way it works is that a company offers a discount on a product or service and if a predetermined minimum number of users opt in for the deal, everyone gets the deal. If the minimum is not met, no one gets it. The drawback for small businesses is that the response can be too overwhelming to meet demand—thus generating negative PR.

Offline

Finally, many of the offline channels are still perennial favorites for marketing and promotion and are so embedded in our culture that we don't feel we really need to define or comment too heavily on them:

- word-of-mouth
- physical location/attractive signage
- radio advertising (terrestrial or satellite)
- local TV/cable advertising
- sponsoring community events

Putting It All Together

We've given you a lot of ideas in this chapter for promoting and marketing your home business. The channels—and combination of channels—you ultimately choose will depend, on your budget, your expertise, the time you have available, and the types of customers you are trying to reach. In fact, you may have a steady stream of clients that you have acquired through traditional networking or other means and may not need to avail yourself of *any* these channels. And, of course, if you are a teleworker for a parent company, they have a whole marketing department and/or ad agency that handles all of these issues.[17]

Our advice is to draw up a list of maybe a half dozen channels you would *definitely* find helpful for promoting your type of business and that you would be able to begin using immediately. That is, you are reasonably knowledgeable and have the time and budget to start right away. We're thinking social media, a blog, etc. You can start with the list of channels provided in this chapter.

After that, identify another half dozen that you are interested in, but would require additional budget, or time, or expertise that might be *slightly* out of your grasp, a wish list, if you will.

That gives you a dozen channels to play with. Start with the

---

[17] There can also be some overlap. Individual financial advisors, for example, may be employed by a large wealth management corporation like Merrill Lynch but may need to market themselves directly to potential customers.

easy ones, and as time and resources permit, investigate the not-so-easy ones. Just remember the most important rule of multichannel marketing: consistency of brand identity and marketing message across all of these channels.

MEASURE FOR MEASURE: CHOOSE YOUR METRICS

Decide what your metrics for success will be. In other words, what will you consider effective marketing, and what will you consider a waste of time and money? Four new customers/projects in six months? One good, high-quality project a year? A certain amount of revenue growth per month? Whatever metric you choose, make sure that it's realistic. In the world of social media, metrics are murky, and there is no standard measure of what is effective and successful. Regardless, also make sure that you have been as diligent and persistent as possible before you declare something a failure. If you fail to update a blog for six months and then find you have no comments and site traffic is non-existent, well, maybe the problem is your own lack of effort. If social media is not paying off in any way, perhaps you are not active enough. Are you posting things regularly? Are you adding contacts? Joining groups? Think of it as going to an in-person networking function and spending the whole time sitting at the bar with your back to the crowd until everyone is gone. Would you wonder why you didn't make any contacts?

Moving Forward

In many ways, this chapter has included a lot of topics that can actually be fun—coming up with marketing and promotion plans, playing around with social media, networking, etc. In the next chapter, we'll look at some of the less fun aspects of a home business: dealing with matters like health insurance, tax planning, accounting, and ensuring you get paid.

To Do:

❑ Identify the various collateral materials you'll need. Business cards? Letterhead? Envelopes/mailing labels?

❑ Get to work developing your company website, either by doing it yourself or hiring a web designer. Make sure you purchase a good domain name for your business.

❑ Think about how you would want to market your business. Whom are you trying to reach, and what would likely be the best way of reaching them?

❑ Unless you have a compelling reason not to, become active in the "Big Three" social media—Facebook, LinkedIn, and Twitter. Create and refine a good profile, and develop a schedule for posting regular updates and engaging in other activities.

❑ Consider taking advantage of some of LinkedIn's new services, such as Slideshare or Pulse, or services like branded.me that uses Linked In profiles as the basis of personal websites.

❑ Review our list of media channels. Identify five or six channels you would be comfortable implementing immediately and another five or six for your "wish list."

❑ Decide what your metrics for success will be—based on realistic expectations. What results in what time period would you consider a success vs. a failure? And if a failure occurs, be honest about what the problems might have been. Too little activity on your own part? The wrong kind of activity? Before abandoning an idea completely, see if, with a little retooling or extra effort, it could be made to pay off.

CHAPTER 7

Health and Taxes

"I'm proud to be paying taxes in the United States. The only thing is I could be just as proud for half the money."

—Arthur Godfrey, radio and TV broadcaster

"I detest life insurance agents; they always argue that I shall some day die, which is not so."

—Stephen Leacock, humorist and writer

Answer These Questions:

Do you have a business attorney? An accountant? A bookkeeper?

Do you know the difference between a sole proprietorship, an S corporation, and a limited liability company (LLC)? Which might be the best option for your business?

How do you plan to manage your business accounts?

Do you know the difference between profit and cashflow?

Do you have a business bank account? A business credit card?

Do you know how to collect from "deadbeat" clients?

Do you know how to estimate taxes?

What are your health insurance needs?

What other insurance might you need?

Many aspects of working from home are actually a lot of fun. Depending on how you feel about the work you do, you may find your day-to-day tasks highly enjoyable. After all, why do something you don't enjoy?

That said, there are a number of serious matters that need to be addressed but aren't particularly enjoyable. And while some people find making money to be enjoyable, the logistics of moving that money around and keeping track of it might not be for many of us. In particular, the outflow of money is far less enjoyable than the inflow.

In this chapter, let's look at the movement and tracking of money. But first, you need to make some big-picture decisions about your business that will affect much of that money movement.

What Type of Business Are You?

If you work from home, it is tempting to think that just by turning on the computer, doing work, and getting paid for it, you are—*voilà!*—a business. And in general, from the perspective of your day-to-day life, that's true. But for tax purposes, you may need to make some decisions about how your business should be classified. We don't mean in terms of industry or market (writer, hairdresser, plumber), but rather your business *structure*. There are a number of options from which to choose, but in the majority of cases, a home business will be a *sole proprietorship*. Setting yourself up as another kind of business entity may make more sense from a financial and practical standpoint, however. The decisions you make at this point can have substantial tax benefits down the road—or may create substantial bookkeeping and other challenges that can be disruptive to the basic tasks that comprise your business. This is why we strongly suggest you sit down with a professional at the outset—not someone at a tax preparation service like H&R Block—and carefully review your options.

SEEK PROFESSIONAL ADVICE

We hasten to add that what we discuss in this chapter should not be construed as any kind of substitute for professional advice. As we say in Chapter 1, and elsewhere throughout this book, there is such a wide variety of businesses that you may be involved in, and such a wide variety of personal and professional circumstances, that we can only speak in the most general of terms. As a result, there are two, maybe three, appointments you will want to set up before you hang out your shingle:

- *Business Attorney.* Remember the zoning conversation from Chapter 1? Your attorney can help you determine if zoning is an issue. Your lawyer will also help decide what kind of business you should be (corporation, S corporation, LLC, etc.—see below), and help with issues pertaining to liability and lawsuits. S/he can help you draw up contracts to use with clients, advise about intellectual property (copyrights, patents, and trademarks), and even assist in collections (see below). Lawyers, like doctors, are becoming increasingly specialized, and even though "business lawyer" may already sound fairly specialized, individual attorneys may specialize in only contracts, or real estate, or intellectual property, or licenses, or...well, you get the picture. You may have to hunt around if you are looking for a "general purpose" business lawyer. As always, the best way to find one may well be word–of–mouth, seeking advice from colleagues or other businesses you may know, Chambers of Commerce, or the Small Business Association.

- *Accountant.* At the very least, a good accountant will handle all your tax preparation, will know what is deductible and what is not, be up-to-date on the latest tax law changes, and will take care of all the federal, state, and local filing requirements. At best, s/he will also periodically review your accounts (the "books"), make sure you are estimating your taxes correctly (more on this later), make sure all expenses are are categorized correctly, make sure there is no duplication, advise on investing and retirement planning, do billing, and just handle everything that Quicken or QuickBooks (see below) cannot. As a small home business, your accounting needs will probably be modest, and if you have only one employee (yourself), that simplifies things greatly. But as your business grows, your books may become more complicated and time-consuming to manage, and you may need an accountant or a bookkeeper (see next item) to free you up to do your actual productive work. A good accountant is found in the same way as you would find a lawyer, and especially when you are trusting someone with your finances, personal referrals may be even more vitally important here. One of the key reasons to find an accountant is that they are often more knowledgeable about filings, permits, and the like than lawyers are because local accountants have many small customers. You want an *accountant*, not just a tax preparer.

- *Bookkeeper.* You may even find it helpful to hire a bookkeeper to come in once a month or so and go over your books and make sure everything is in order. A freelance bookkeeper can be less expensive than hiring a full-fledged CPA or accountant.

Accountants vs. Bookkeepers

What is the difference between an accountant and a bookkeeper? It could be said it is a matter of degrees. A proper "accountant" typically has a four-year college degree, usually from a business school. Large companies hire in-house accountants to handle or oversee the company finances. A Certified Public Accountant (CPA), as the name suggests, not only has been schooled in business and accounting but must also pass the Uniform Certified Public Accountant Examination as well as various state requirements. CPAs typically set up their own accounting firms, but they may also serve in the role of a company's in-house accountant, either full-time or on a freelance basis. Bookkeepers generally lack the extensive education of an accountant or CPA and function more as clerks than as financial advisors. They can maintain accounting records, keep track of income and outgo, generate invoices and checks, handle payroll, and other basic tasks. As a home business owner, you may yourself be what would be considered a bookkeeper. There are various training and certification programs for bookkeepers, but the requirements are not as stringent as for CPAs.

BUSINESS CLASSIFICATIONS

Your lawyer and/or accountant can advise you on how to structure your business, but here are the general classifications:

- *Sole Proprietorship.* This will likely be how your home business will be set up—at least at first. As the term indicates, this is a business owned and operated by one individual (you); there is no legal, or perhaps even financial, distinction between the owner and the business. You get all the profits, but you are also responsible for all losses and debts. It is also common for sole proprietorships to report income on the owner's personal income tax forms, with the appropriate Schedule(s) (SE, C, E, etc.) attached.[1] Information about sole proprietorships vis-à-vis taxes can be found at the IRS's website.[2]

- *Partnership.* You may be going into your home business either by yourself (sole proprietorship) or with one or more partners. In a home business, that partner may be your spouse or some other relation, but it may also be one or more business partners unrelated to you. In an official, legal partnership, each partner contributes money, property, work or some skill to the business and as a result is entitled to share the profits—and expected to share the losses—of the business. The exact terms of the partnership—who contributes what, who receives what, etc.—will be drawn up by your business attorney. Taxwise, a partnership files an "information return" to report income, deductions, gains, and losses, but income tax is only paid by the individual partners on their personal tax returns. Information about partnerships vis-à-vis taxes can be found at the IRS's website.[3]

---

[1] If you file your incomes taxes jointly with a spouse, you would report your income the same way you would if you had a full-time job. It gets complicated when your spouse has a controlling interest in the business, in which case it may either be a joint venture or a partnership. If this situation seems like it applies to you, talk to your accountant, or start at http://1.usa.gov/1s81BlF.

[2] See http://1.usa.gov/1qVeNth.

[3] See http://1.usa.gov/1vU8l7F.

- *Corporation/C Corporation.* In this kind of business, "shareholders" invest in the business and in return receive shares of the corporation's capital stock.[4] The corporation—more specifically a C corporation—does its business, earns revenue, pays expenses, is responsible for taxes, and distributes whatever profits there may be to the shareholders. Corporate profits are taxed, and when distributed to shareholders as dividends are taxed again. Information about corporations with respect to taxes can be found at the IRS website.[5] As a small home business, you may not see any real advantage in incorporating your business. However, there is a scaled-down version called an S corporation that may be appropriate for you.

- *S Corporation.* An S corporation is a hybrid of a sole proprietorship and a corporation, and a sole proprietor can set up his or her business as an S corporation. Income, losses, and deductions are passed through to the corporation's shareholder (i.e., you), who then reports income and losses on his or her personal tax return. They also pay taxes at the individual income tax rates, allowing S corporations to avoid double taxation on the corporate income. Information about S corporations in relation to taxes can be found at the IRS's website.[6]

- *Limited Liability Company (LLC).* A Limited Liability Company (LLC) is a corporation and partnership/sole proprietorship hybrid. An LLC is not incorporated, although the one feature it shares with a corporation is the limited liability of its members (the partners or proprietors in an LLC are called members), which means that, unlike a sole proprietorship or a partnership, the business is a separate entity, and the mem-

---

[4] This stock can either be private (i.e., only exchanged among a small, controlled pool of investors) or public (the stock is listed on a stock exchange and anyone can buy shares).
[5] See http://1.usa.gov/1q2pcWD.
[6] See http://1.usa.gov/1nNwRnq.

bers are shielded legally and financially from the business. Taxwise, an LLC features the same kind of pass-through income taxation as a partnership—income, etc., is reported on its members personal tax returns. LLCs can also have a single owner. Each state, however, has its own regulations regarding LLCs. Information about LLCs vis-à-vis taxes can be found at the IRS's website.[7]

- *Independent Contractor.* You may not actually opt to create a business at all and just operate as an independent contractor. That is, you do work-for-hire for companies—such as copywriting, graphic design, or other services—under your own name without considering it a "business" per se. In reality, there may be little real distinction between being an independent contractor and operating as a sole proprietorship.

- *Teleworker.* Finally, the easiest, from both a legal and accounting standpoint, is being a teleworker. This means you are a full-time employee of a parent company, and your only responsibility legally and financially is filing a personal income tax return.

Keep in mind that you don't have to maintain the same business classification forever. As you go on, and as your business grows, you can switch from one type of classification to another say, from a Schedule S-based independent contractor to an S Corporation, or from a sole proprietorship to a proper corporation. Again, sound financial advice can help you make the decision that is best for your circumstances.

---

[7] See http://1.usa.gov/1vvkHUe.

Making—or Keeping—Book

Accounting doesn't need to be excessively complicated. While there are certainly right and wrong ways of doing things,[8] software has made it pretty easy to keep track of income and outgo. And that's really all accounting is: keeping track of things. Or, not to put too fine a point on it, *accounting for things*. As always, there are several different ways of accomplishing this.

Related to accounting is billing, and many higher-end accounting software solutions can help automate the process of invoicing and paying bills, as well as general accounting. For a small home business, anything more elaborate will likely be overkill.

We want to stress that, regardless of which options you choose, the more diligent you are in the day-to-day management of your accounts, the less work you will have to do come April (or whenever your business' fiscal year ends), and the more you will save on tax preparation charges. The best way to handle that is to do it right from the start. A good analogy is to maintain your books the way you should maintain your home. If you have guests coming over or are planning a party, you know that cleaning the house is a massive undertaking if it hasn't been cleaned in four months. On the other hand, if you have been diligent about tidying up on a daily or weekly basis, it's less of a task when there is a hard deadline. The same with accounting and administrative tasks.

Set Up Basic Accounts

You should set up different bank account(s) for your business and not mingle business income and expenses with personal income and expenses, even if they are technically the same. Depending on the type of business you set up earlier, you may not be allowed to. What kind of accounts?

---

[8] Handing a plastic grocery bag full of random receipts—and nothing else—to one's tax accountant on April 14 is decidedly the wrong way to do things.

- *Bank account.* While you may not require a separate savings account, do set up a separate business checking account,[9] and pay any business-related bills from that account.

- *Credit card.* Apply for a separate credit card that you will only use for business expenses.[10]

Another reason to set up a separate business bank account is, again, for professional reasons. When clients pay you, it will most likely be by check, and if you lump everything in your personal bank account, clients will have to make checks out to you personally, not your business name. That's not a calamity, but it makes you look a bit less professional and can create logistical problems at your bank when people make out checks using your company name.[11]

MANUAL ACCOUNTING

If you've read Charles Dickens novels, or seen any film or TV adaptations of them, characters were always working in counting houses, jotting figures in ledgers using quill pens. Well, that's still an option for keeping your books—keeping literal, actual books, even if not using quill pens anymore. Ledger books do still exist and allow you to set up different pages for different things—income, expenses, expenses by classification, and so forth.

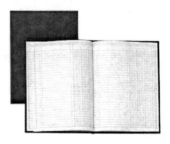

This is certainly one way to do it, and you may actually be more comfortable doing your accounting manually. If you have very simple needs, ledger books might suit them perfectly. But if your

---

[9] In this age of online banking, the idea of a "checking" account may seem like a quaint notion, but essentially you want an account you can use to pay expenses. For the foreseeable future, it is advisable to have it be a checking account, as there are still quite a few occasions when paying by check is the most convenient—or only possible—option.
[10] Inevitably, you will occasionally need to use a personal card for business expenses if, for example, your business card is an American Express card and someone doesn't take AmEx.
[11] Banks are a bit more lax these days, especially if you have a good relationship with your bank manager.

business grows and you can ill afford the time and labor of doing everything manually, you can explore software options.

SPREADSHEET SOFTWARE

A general purpose spreadsheet program like Microsoft Excel (or the LibreOffice equivalent) can also function perfectly well as an accounting program. Spreadsheet files comprise different worksheets, which can be set up to track different transactions. One can serve as a general check register/passbook for your business account, another can track expenses using different columns for different categories of expenses, like "postage/shipping," "insurance," "office supplies," "travel," "utilities," and so forth. Another worksheet can track your billing and outstanding invoices (a useful thing to track), while another can track your year-to-date (YTD) income. If you are proficient at writing formulas in Excel, you can have it warn you when you are exceeding the income level on which your estimated tax payments have been based (see below), which can help you adjust what you pay the IRS and your state quarterly.

At the end of the year, it's easy to sum up all the columns, and hand either the file or a printout to your tax accountant.

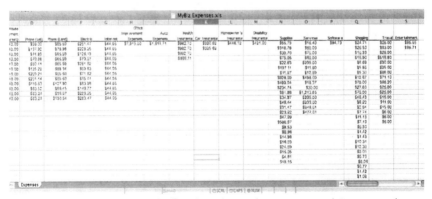

A basic spreadsheet program like Excel can be easily set up to track income and outgo, and track expenses by category.

QUICKEN/QUICKBOOKS

The most popular "consumer"-level account software programs are Quicken and its sister QuickBooks. What is the difference? QuickBooks has more features, lets you add more detail about individual transactions,

Finance software like Quicken is good for managing your business account.

has a payroll system, supports more than one user, supports double-entry accounting, and costs $150 and up vs. about $50 for Quicken. For most small businesses with fairly modest accounting needs, Quicken will likely suffice, but take a look at a comparison of features[12] to determine if one would suit your needs better than the other. Keep in mind that, generally, Quicken is designed more for sole proprietorships and requires various workarounds if you need to measure the net worth of your business.

Alternatives to Quicken

Although Quicken and QuickBooks are the most popular software packages, there are many others. A selection of comparative reviews can be found at http://bit.ly/1nN2eNw, which has been updated to include 2015 offerings. There are also online accounting services such as Zoho (www.zoho.com), one advantage of which is that all documents and files are stored in the cloud on their servers, which means you don't need to keep them stored locally on your own computer. The Gold Award Winner for 2015 was Fresh Books Cloud Acccounting.

TRACKING INCOME AND EXPENSES

You can use accounting software to track your income and expenses—what's come in and what's gone out. You can run a monthly report that will track your income and subtract your outgo to give you an idea of your profitability, or at the very least your cashflow.

---

[12] See http://bit.ly/1yn9a7K.

Billing

Billing should be a simple process (unlike collecting, see below), and for most businesses it is. Essentially, you create an invoice for services rendered or products purchased, depending upon your business.

Invoicing can be as low-tech as a pad of invoice sheets, or as high-tech as electronic bills auto-generated from an account management system—to everything in between. If you're a small home business, you probably don't have enough volume of work that billing is a massive undertaking. An invoice template in Microsoft Word (or the program of your choice) will likely suffice. An invoice should include some basic elements:

- Your company logo (it's technically marketing collateral).

- Address to which to send payment.

- Your contact information should there be an issue or question.[13]

- Invoice date.

- Invoice number. This convention is just for your own internal bookkeeping, and can use any system you like. It can be simply chronological (1001, 1002, etc.), or perhaps include the date and a client code. If you billed a company called My Customer on April 1, 2013, your invoice number could simply be MC13-0401. This can make it easy to sort invoice files or numbers by client and year, if necessary.

- Brief description of work performed or the project name.

- The amount you are charging for the work. If you are billing on an hourly basis, it is customary to also include the number of hours and the hourly rate—"8 hrs @ $100/hr," for example.

- Other items being invoiced.

- Total amount.

[13] Actually, you should use your company letterhead for invoices.

Cashflow vs. Profit

We think we know what "profit" means: income minus expenses. Take your income over a certain period—say, one year. Assume it was $100,000. Now add up all your expenses over that same period. Assume all your business-related expenses were $40,000. Subtract total expenses from your income and that $60,000 can be said to be your profit. (It can get more complicated than this, but you get the idea.) On the other hand, if the scenario were reversed, and yearly income was $40,000 with yearly expenses of $100,000—doing the subtraction would yield -$60,000, which would be your loss, the opposite of profit. (Businesses often look at P&L—Profit and Loss—statements to figure out if the company is running in the black or in the red.)

Cashflow, on the other hand, refers to how much actual money is flowing through your bank account. Over the course of a month, one client sends you a check for $2,500, another client sends you a check for $1,500, and another client $1,000. In that month, you had $5,000 physically appear in your bank account. In that same month, you had various expenses that totaled $2,500. So that's a net of +$2,500—a positive cashflow, we would say. Again, flip the figures, and if your deposits subtracted by your expenses came out to -$2,500, that would be negative cashflow.

Over a period of time, you can have profits, but not necessarily cashflow. Let's see how.

Profit can exist on paper (or in Quicken) before it manifests itself as cash—and in some industries, this is more acute than in others. Think about it this way.

Your company bills a client $5,000 on April 1 for a project you completed in March. Technically, that can be recorded as revenue. The invoice was dated April 1, so perhaps your client thought it was a joke, and didn't pay it until you reminded them a month later on May 1. In the meantime, you had expenses in April of $2,500. On paper, you billed $5,000 and had expenses of $2,500, which indicates a profit of $2,500. But in terms of actual money flowing through your bank account, you had $0 income, but $2,500 in expenses—negative cashflow.

Accrual accounting looks at profit in terms of what has been billed and paid over a period of time, treating what has been billed as income, while *cash accounting* focuses on actual money that has physically been received and spent at a specific point in time. As a small business, you will want to focus more on cash accounting than accrual accounting, but the latter is common in larger corporate enterprises, usually retail.

A basic invoice can be generated using Word's "Invoice" template or created/ customized in the program of your choice.

- "Net 30 days." This is supposed to indicate that the customer has thirty calendar days to pay the invoice. Whether this is legally binding is open to debate, but as a small business you have little affordable legal recourse, and most companies you work with probably have a standard window between receiving an invoice and paying it, a window which seems to open wider every year. Still, it might be a nice stimulant.

- Bank routing number(s). Clients, especially those overseas, may prefer to pay you electronically, so including the routing numbers required for electronic wire transfers will be necessary.

If you are invoicing for reimbursement of expenses, be sure to attach copies of the salient receipts. If you are submitting invoices electronically, printed invoices can be scanned with a document scanner or even photographed with a smartphone camera.[14]

[14] Yes, there is an app for that. Abukai Expenses, to name but one, is an iPhone app that

Invoices can be printed and mailed, but sending invoices as PDFs via e-mail is largely the way billing is done these days.

Getting Paid

It may sound like one of Newton's Laws of Motion, and maybe it should be: for every account payable there should be an equal and opposite account receivable. That is, every invoice should result in a check.

As we said earlier, billing is easy, collecting is—or can be—difficult. We would estimate that, seven or eight times out of ten, you will not have a significant problem receiving payment, and maybe, of those three or four problem clients, two or three of them will simply just be later than you would prefer. Maybe the client is waiting for one of their own clients to pay  them before they can pay you, and so forth. But what about those one or two times when you really are dealing with, to be frank, deadbeats?

First of all, *don't be shy* about requesting payment. People running small businesses are often concerned about offending a customer if they persist in trying to collect an overdue invoice. But look: *they're* the one doing the offending. You did work that was accepted. You lived up to your end of the bargain; *they're* the ones who reneged on the deal. And let's face it: if they refuse to pay you, do you really want to do work for them again?

Here's a timeline for dealing with overdue payments.

- *T plus 30 days from invoice mail date.* "Net 30 days" is the standard payment period, unless you have specifically negotiated (or been cajoled into agreeing to) a longer pay period. If payment has not been received in thirty days after the invoice was mailed (although it is common to exclude "transit

---

lets you take pictures of receipts with your phone's camera, and it will automatically process them into an expense report.

time" in the thirty-day window), rebill. Send an exact copy of the original invoice with "Second Notice" in prominent red letters. Don't be obnoxious with the typography, but ensure that it is clearly noticeable. Request that payment be remitted "upon receipt."[15]

- *T plus 37 days.* If still no payment within a week, send an e-mail to the client gently and politely pointing out that payment still has not been received. Suggest that perhaps the check is already in the mail. It's probably not, but at least giving them the benefit of the (lack of) doubt may help lubricate the accounts payable department.

- *T plus 40 days.* If your e-mail has been ignored, pick up the phone. Call the client. Again, be friendly and courteous, but firm. Do the same if you have to leave a voicemail. Calling a client to collect money is one of the toughest things a small business owner may have to do, but at times it's a necessary evil. Also, never apologize. You have no reason to apologize; they're late.

- *T plus 45 days.* If you spoke to the client, and s/he said the check was on its way, and there still is no check received after a generous five days—or if your voicemail was ignored—start getting tough. If you have an attorney, have him send the client a letter. You'd be surprised what a lawyer's letterhead alone can accomplish. Sure, you may end up paying your lawyer's hourly rate, but depending on the outstanding invoice amount, it may be worth it. (There are also collection agencies, but when you work with them you only get a small portion of what is collected, so only use them as a last resort.)

- *T plus 50+ days.* If *that* doesn't work, start the proceedings to take the client to small claims court. Chances are they'll settle out of court.

---

[15] Some would argue that all invoices should be stamped "payable upon receipt," and it's hard to argue with that.

Refuse to accept partial payments. Doing so sets a bad precedent, and the partial amount may be all you ever get.

Stay away from barter arrangements; you could create unintentional tax issues. It's one thing to do a favor now and then or as professional courtesy. But bartering deals can create some IRS issues. It's better off to buy services from each other, even if it seems like you are just "trading dollars."

That all said, depending on the amount owed, it may just be more worth your while to write it off and move on. Just never pass up the opportunity to warn any colleagues not to work with this individual or company.

> ## In Our Experience: Early Bird Discounts
>
> One way to avoid the problem of not getting paid is to offer a discount for payment up front. In Dr. Joe's consulting practice, he offered a ten-percent discount if clients paid in advance, or upon signing the work agreement contract. It often can be worth the lower price, in terms of cashflow, and in terms of avoiding a collection problem later. Newer clients may be hesitant to pay before they see any work done, but often clients with whom you have worked before may be more amenable.

Bounced Checks

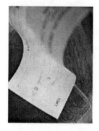

Dealing with bounced checks is related to the non-payment issue. Every once in a while, you will get a check that doesn't clear. In some cases, it may just be an oversight or a case of bad timing. If your client is an individual (as opposed to a corporation), s/he might not keep a large balance in their checking accounts (because such paltry interest, if any, is earned) and only transfer funds from a high-interest rate savings or money market account when there are bills to be paid. If the timing is off, or someone forgets to make a transfer, there can be an overdraft. In most cases, the check can just be redeposited, and all's well that ends well.

If the check keeps bouncing like a rubber ball, however, request a certified or cashier's check. If that is not forthcoming, revisit the timeline above.

What To Bill?

As you were reading about the mechanics of billing, you probably had the question, "What amount should I bill for my services?" Whenever we meet someone who is starting their own business, beginning to do freelance work on the side, or adding an entirely new service, that's one of the first questions they have. If you quote too high a cost, you may lose the business to sticker shock, but if you charge too little, you may not make enough to cover expenses or even make it worth your professional while. It can be quite a conundrum. And clients are always coy about what they are willing to pay—they don't want to end up paying more than they have to, and they're afraid of suggesting a price much higher than *you* were thinking, because of course you'll take that instead. So that's *their* conundrum.

And the answer is...it depends. That's a mushy response, but even in industries and markets with which we are familiar, there are few standard rates for services. Some things to think about when quoting rates, though:

- Remember that any project, no matter how little or now much you charge, has an opportunity cost associated with it. That means that the time you are putting into one project is time you can't put into another project, perhaps a higher paying one. That opportunity cost should not dwarf what you end up getting for a project.

- Be sure you cover your expenses. If the project for which you are quoting a price will require a specific outlay for supplies or other services (paper, printing or copying, binding, whatever), estimate those expenses the best you can and use that estimate as a starting point. Add twenty or thirty percent on top of that as the lowest range of your estimate.

- If you have friends or close associates who do similar work, ask them what they charge.

- If you have a standard hourly rate that you use for all clients, use that. Others have been willing to pay it, so it's obviously not out of line.

- Get as accurate an estimate of the scope of the project and what will be required as possible. It's not always easy to gauge how much work something is going to be, but don't be afraid to mentally apply a "PITA surcharge" to any quote. PITA stands for "Pain In The A--," and there's nothing wrong with PITA projects. After all, that which doesn't kill us only makes us stronger—just make sure you're adequately compensated for the anguish.

- Don't be afraid to sound expensive, as it makes you sound more professional or that you are highly skilled and knowledgeable (which of course you are). If you come off sounding dirt cheap, clients will assume they're going to get what they pay for.

- Do a little research on the client. Are they a big corporation that probably has a few bucks, or are they small and likely more budget-constrained?

- Once you pick a number, suggest that there may be some room to negotiate. Even knocking ten percent off what you quoted may still be better than losing the client entirely. After all, it may lead to a new long-term relationship that can lead to steady work in the future.

- *Don't do anything for free.* It has become increasingly common to have companies ask you to blog or provide content for free or, more insidiously, "for the exposure." Unless you're doing a favor for a friend, don't get in the habit of doing work for free.

- Don't be afraid to let some jobs go. If it sounds like it will require far more work than the customer is willing to pay for, it may be best to just skip it.

Deciding what to charge a client can be one of the most difficult tasks in running a business, and truth be told it does involve a great deal of trial and error and floating trial balloons.

Square: Turn Your Smartphone into a Bank

One way of avoiding the problem of checks either not appearing or bouncing is to accept credit cards. Historically, it has not been easy or inexpensive for small companies, especially sole proprietorships, to set up merchant accounts to do so.

One solution we want to highlight is called Square (https://squareup.com/). It comprises an app and corresponding hardware reader that lets you accept credit card payments through an iPhone or iPad. You connect the reader to the phone or tablet, swipe a credit card, and *voilà*! Someone has just easily purchased something from you. The app is linked to your bank account without having to go through the pain and expense of setting

up a merchant account with a credit card company. The app is free, and the only fee is a 2.75-percent swipe fee for each transaction. Alternately, you can pay a flat $275 annual fee if that would work out more economically. By the way, all financial transaction information is saved on Square's secure servers, not anywhere on the device, so you don't need to fret if your phone is ever lost or stolen. (Well, at least you don't have to fret about Square.) Square also lets you automatically charge the appropriate sales tax. Square offers a large number of additional features and services and is worth checking out if your business will require a lot of in-person payments. Of course, you always face the chance that the client's card will be rejected. Sometimes there is just no winning. By the way, Square is constantly evolving their services, and now offer point-of-sale stands and even contactless readers to accept payments via ApplePay as well as new chip cards. Square also offers a wide range of fianancial tools and services for a variety of business types.

PayPal is another option for small businesses, and you can set up a Merchant Account. Investigate PayPal at www.paypal.com.

Tax Planning

Nobody likes paying taxes, but then no one likes paying their electric bill, their phone bill, or...well, people just don't like paying bills at all, and it's not hard to see why. Although many of our bills, like a rent or mortgage, are a fixed amount we pay every month no matter what, many we can strive to reduce. We can turn the heat down in the winter and the A/C down in the summer to save electricity. We can control our calling and data usage to lower our cellphone bills, and we can downgrade our cable service to lower our monthly cost. So, too, can you strive to lower your tax bill.

What Do You Owe?

The first question you may have your first year in operation is, "What do I even owe?" You owe federal income tax, state income tax (if your state has a state income tax)[16], as well as "self-employment tax." This latter tax is a substitute for the withholding tax— FICA (Social Security) and Medicare—you and your employer would pay if you were a salaried employee. And like the taxes you would pay if you were a salaried employee, what you owe is based on your Adjusted Gross Income (AGI), which is the starting point for all tax planning. Your AGI is— simply defined, but not always simply calculated—your total income minus any adjustments, such as deductions, exemptions, contributions to an IRA, etc.

Make Less, Keep More

In 2015, when Dr. Joe did a series of working-at-home workshop presentations, attendees were shocked when they heard about the double payment of Social Security taxes. They thought they made a dollar in profit—but they really only made 84.7 cents. When they put money into an IRA or an HSA, it's like they instantly made 15.3 percent on their money (actually it's better than that—18 percent—because it's based on the 84.7 cents. And then it compounds from there tax-free). This is part of a "make less, keep more" strategy.

Deductions

Deductions include all the legitimate business expenses you incurred over the course of the year. They can include, but are not limited to:

- A percentage of your rent or mortgage, if a dedicated portion of your home was used for business purposes which, if you are reading this book, it is. The percentage that is deductible should be equal to the percentage of your home that is used for business. So it's a good idea if you have the architectural plan for the home to note the total square footage, and then the square footage of the rooms involved, and keep that figure in your records.[17]

- A percentage of your utility bills (phone, Internet, electric, etc.). Utilities can be allocated by square footage. It's always

[16] Some cities may also impose a local income tax, as well.
[17] You can start at the IRS's website for the Home Office Deduction at http://1.usa. gov/18v4jL9.

better to have a separate phone and Internet account. If that's not possible or practical, allocate them by use. Just keep a log for a few months, and then you can develop a reasonable percentage that you can apply in the future.

- Some percentage of any auto repair, maintenance, or gas expenses, if you use your car substantially for business travel other than commuting. That is, unless you reimburse yourself for mileage based on the standard IRS mileage rate. As of this writing, it is 56 cents per mile, which is supposed to cover all of the costs of running a vehicle. Some businesses, such as a plumber, for example, have a separate vehicle just for business. In such cases, all of the costs are deductible.

- Office supplies, furniture, computers[18], hardware and software, and anything else you bought for your office.

- A Post Office or UPS Store box you use as your business address.

- Shipping and postage that was used for business purposes.

- Travel expenses.

- A percentage of entertainment expenses, such as taking a client out to lunch or dinner or some other event, such as a Broadway show, golf game, etc.

- Capital improvements to your office.

- Health insurance premiums.

- Start-up costs, like office furniture and equipment, computer hardware and software, office supplies, any construction undertaken to create your office space, and any other expenses related to getting your business or office set up.

---

[18] If you use a single computer for both personal and business computing, technically you should not deduct one hundred percent of the cost of the computer as a business expense. The same goes for anything else you may buy, although you don't have to get too crazy. You can use some paper clips for personal use but deduct the cost of the whole box of paper clips.

You Do the Math!

In order to determine what percentage of your home expenses can be allocated to your home office, you should determine, as precisely as possible, how much of your home is devoted to your workspace. Let's do the math.

First, get a layout plan of your house and mark off where your office space will be. For example, in the floor plan here, Bedroom 2 and Bedroom 3, demarcated by the dashed lines, are the designated office space.

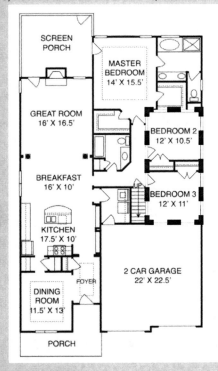

Determine the square footage of your house. The total official square footage is often on your property tax bill, or on whatever real estate documents and materials you used when you bought the house. If you have an apartment, your landlord may know, or you may be forced to get out a tape measure. In this case, the total area is 2,450 square feet.

Calculate the square footage of your house dedicated to your office space. On the floor plan, you can see that Bedroom 2 is 12 x 10.5 feet and Bedroom 3 is 12 x 11 feet. That makes the total office space 12 feet x 21.5 feet, or 258 square feet. (Don't forget to include attic or basement storage if necessary.)

Calculate the percentage of your total square footage dedicated to your office space. In this case, that would be 258 ÷ 2,450 = 10.5 percent.

Use that calculation to reimburse your expenses, such as utilities like electricity, gas (for heating, if applicable), etc.

Take pictures of your office and storage space, and keep documentation in a safe place. Create a document with the images, layout, and calculation and save it as a PDF. Store it in the cloud so you can always find it, and give a copy to your accountant with your tax information.

You get the idea. This is why you need a good accounting system to keep track of all of these expenses and classify them by type. As you can see, some types of expenses are completely deductible, while others are only partially deductible. Your accountant can give you a much clearer idea about the deductibility of various business expenses that specifically relate to your own situation and business type.

Contributions

Another way of reducing your AGI is by contributing to an IRA or other retirement account (see below). It's a good idea to contribute yearly to a retirement account like an IRA anyway, but that the amount of the contribution lowers your AGI is a happy benefit.

FILING ESTIMATED TAXES

Once you and your accountant have determined what your AGI is likely to be for the first year you are in business, you can use the IRS's (and your state's) tax tables to figure out your liability. Most small businesses file quarterly; so you would pay one-fourth of your tax liability by April 15, one-fourth by June 15, one-fourth by September 15, and one-fourth by January 15 of the following year. Again, this is essentially what would happen if you were a salaried employee; in that case, it would be called withholding tax. It's the same basic concept, but a) you are withholding our own taxes and, b) as an independent contractor without a regular salary, your income can only really be estimated, at least as far as the IRS is concerned.[19]

> **In Our Experience: Don't Underestimate Taxes**
>
> Although your overall tax bill will be the same whether you pay it in quarterly installments or all in one go in April, you may not have the cashflow in April to pay a huge amount in one fell swoop. So it's preferable—financially and psychologically—to pay a little extra attention to your estimated tax payments. Trust us on this. The first year of self-employment can be quite an eye-opener if you underestimate your taxes!

[19] You may actually know what your yearly income is, if you have steady clients and regular projects that have all been contracted and budgeted, or if you are on a retainer for a fixed fee payable at regular intervals.

1099 Red Balloons

When/if you were a salaried employee, you filled out a W-4 form for your company's HR department. At the beginning of every year, your employer gave you a W-2 form which you submitted with your tax return. Since you are now self-employed, you will no longer get a W-2.

What you *will* get, usually, are 1099s. Each of the companies for whom you did work will (or should) mail you a 1099 form that tells you how much you were paid. The legal deadline for sending these is the January 31 following the end of the tax year being reported. Always doublecheck your 1099s against your own records, in case someone made an accounting error. You don't want to pay taxes on an amount that is more than you actually received. If the amount is less than you received, you may think you're putting one over on Uncle Sam. What it really means is that your client will pay more taxes, as they will be reporting a smaller deduction for their services.

Technically, you don't have to submit 1099 forms to the IRS, and not all companies are diligent about sending them out. As long as you declare the income you received, it doesn't matter if you have the form or not.

Make sure companies that hire you know that you are a 1099 employee. Apply for a separate employee identification number (EIN) from the IRS for your business, so you do not have to use your social security number with clients. When you submit your invoice to them, attach a form W-9 which shows this EIN. The client will use this form to set you up as a vendor in their accounting system. It's always easier when this gets set up correctly at the beginning rather than trying to fix it at tax time.

If you have hired any independent contractors and paid them more than $600, you will need to supply *them* with a 1099 form by January 31 following the end of the tax year in which you hired them. When you hire them, be sure to have them fill out a corresponding W-9 form. See the IRS Web site for more information and to obtain forms. There is also a service called filetaxes.com for sending 1099s. It does the automatic filing to the IRS, as well as sending the forms to the contractors. It also can save time and money compared to buying and printing the forms yourself.

If, like many independent contractors and small businesses, your income fluctuates wildly, it is a good idea to track your year-to-date (YTD) income and compare it to what you estimated as your AGI. This way, if you are drastically under what you projected your income to be, you can reduce the amount of your estimated tax payments. Likewise, if it turns out that business is much better than you were expecting, and you are far above your projections, you will want to increase the amount you send in quarterly to avoid being shocked by a nasty tax bill the following April.

Generally speaking, the first year is the most difficult one. After all, you have no idea what to expect for income. In subsequent years, though, you can take the first year as a baseline and calculate new AGIs and thus estimated payments based on the extent to which you see your business growing. And, as we recommended, keep track of how you are doing relative to the previous year and adjust your estimated payments accordingly.

One other caveat is to look at your projected expenses as well as projected income. If you made a large capital investment, bought a new computer, or had other expenses like start-up costs in your first year that will not be typical or repeated in subsequent years, you will end up having a larger  tax burden the following year even if your income stays the same. This happens because those purchases will not be repeated in the second year of operations in most circumstances.

One of the benefits of setting your business up as a corporation is to use a payroll service such as Paychex that will take care of your withholding and make sure the tax deposits are made on time. Their service is relatively inexpensive compared to doing it yourself when you could be working on your business.

A product like Quicken can also help you tax plan quite effectively. Before the end of the year, you can "do your taxes" on a preliminary basis and have a discussion with your accountant about how to minimize them. Very often, when you are a corporation, it is best to show zero profit and take the profits as payroll. It may seem that you are paying more taxes; remember, you are paying both the employee and the employer share of Social Security and Medicare tax, plus federal and state income taxes.

But by taking your built-up cash as payroll, you can reduce your taxes by funding your . Money deposited into 401(k)s, Money Purchase Plans, or Profit Sharing Plans are not taxed until they are withdrawn upon retirement. This is one of the reasons why it's so important to talk to a good accountant.

Sometimes, it's too early to discuss these things until you have an established business. For that reason, it's probably best to start your business as a Sole Proprietorship. Once your business is going with steady work, it's a good time to switch to some kind of corporation.

Savings and IRAs

At least at the outset, most of your income—and whatever funds you had available for start-up costs, like personal savings—will be tied up in running the business and, in fact, it may take some months to see a positive cashflow. As a result, savings and retirement planning may not be the top items on your list of things to worry about, but they're worth thinking about anyway.

We mentioned at the beginning of this chapter that your business should have its own bank account. While we suggested a checking account, you may be better off opening a savings or money market account, which will pay greater interest. Don't expect a massive difference, but if you maintain a large-ish balance, it may end up being substantial over some period of time. Other investment instruments can also generate more yield, if you have the time and the "liquidity" to take advantage of them.

Raw Youth

The age at which you are starting your home business will play a very large role in the extent to which you should worry about IRAs and retirement planning. If you are a student or are in your twenties, there is a bit less urgency, but the fact is that forty sneaks up fairly quickly. You may think you have forever to worry about retirement, but the sooner you get into the habit of stashing funds away for your "golden years," the better they are likely to be.

We know many people who started entirely new businesses on the cusp of sixty, and while it is likely such people have already been contributing to some sort of retirement plan (probably through a full-time job), they'll want to keep contributing to it since life spans are increasing on average every year. Retirement accounts are often the best way to protect your savings against the negative effects of inflation and taxes. Check with your accountant, but the best programs are SEP-IRAs that are deductible from profits, as well as Roth IRAs. The latter come from your pay after taxes, but will never be taxed again, and do not have to be withdrawn by a specific date, according to current law. More details below.

IRAs

If/when you were a salaried employee, chances are you made contributions to a 401(k). As someone who works from home and runs a home business, you no longer have access to a 401(k) and will be required to roll over whatever was in that account into some kind of Individual Retirement Account (IRA).

There are several different types of IRAs:

- *Traditional IRA.* Contributions (the amount you put into it) are often tax-deductible. All intra-IRA transactions and earnings are not taxed, and withdrawals at retirement are taxed as income.

- *Roth IRA.* Contributions are not tax-deductible, but withdrawals are usually tax-free. Still, all transactions within the IRA are not taxed.

- *Keogh plan.* Not really an IRA, but related to it, a Keogh plan is a retirement account for small businesses or the self-employed in which a set amount is automatically contributed every pay period. (There is also a version that can be set up like a profit-sharing plan.) Keogh plans are only applicable to small businesses that have incorporated (see above), not to sole proprietorships or independent contractors.

In all these cases, when you contribute to an IRA, you are contributing to an investment broker's portfolio of some mix of stocks, bonds, mutual funds, and other such instruments. When you meet with a broker to set up such an account, you can choose how "aggressive" you want to be: are you looking for high-risk but potentially quick high-reward stocks, or would you prefer less risk but potentially lower payoff over a longer period of time? Or some middle ground?

Going Broker

Unless you are well-versed in all the nuances involved in investing, you will likely want to consult with a broker, or a financial planner, who can coordinate all your retirement planning and investing. Your business accountant can likely provide recommendations of good financial planners, also called "asset managers," or serve this function him- or herself. Taking advantage of networking opportunities (see Chapter 5) can also introduce you to financial planners, who always seem to be well-represented at those types of events. It couldn't hurt to set up an appointment and pick their brains, especially if you are new to investing. And it is entirely possible that you could get some reciprocal freelance work out of such a meeting as well. Just remember that financial planners have to make money too, and they often sell insurance plans and investment plans that pay them significant commissions. Quite frankly, what they offer is not in your best interests. Like many of the professionals we have discussed throughout this book, word-of-mouth is the best way of finding a good financial planner. Answering a cold call is more than likely not. Paying for a good financial plan that lets you invest and buy yourself may be the best long-term way to reduce costs. It is easier today than ever to set up a disciplined savings plan without commissions and fees.

You aren't limited to IRAs; you can invest in mutual funds, bonds, and stocks directly—if you know what you are doing. Some people are too busy running their businesses and trying to make money by actually working to invest time and energy to following the stock market.[20]

Regardless of what specific financial instruments you choose, you want to contribute enough annually so that you are accruing a meaningful amount, but you don't want to contribute so much that you are adversely affecting your cashflow. Even if your particular plan doesn't impose penalties for early withdrawal, you don't want to get in the habit of raiding your retirement savings to fund current expenses.

Health Insurance

If you ask people who are on the fence about starting a business (or who have started one)—be it a home-based one or not— they will inevitably tell you that the biggest concern and challenge is affording health insurance. Health insurance premiums can be the biggest single expense a business has—and this is before you even get sick. Depending on the type of plan you have, you may be responsible for all sorts of co-pays. If you have a so-called high-deductible plan, in which you pay a relatively low premium, one trip to the emergency room can trigger a seemingly never-ending stream of bills from radiologists, nurses, doctors, etc.

There are a number of things that have changed as a result of the Affordable Care Act (ACA, aka Obamacare). These include:

- Virtually everyone is required to purchase health insurance, although there are exemptions to this rule (see https://www.healthcare.gov/exemptions).

- You can't be denied coverage for a pre-existing condition.

- Children can remain on their parents' health insurance polices until age twenty-six.

---

[20] Funds for retirement can come from anywhere, not necessarily Wall Street. Many people invest in real estate (residential or commercial) which can generate income only if you rent out apartments or office space. Over a long period of time, however, the property value can increase—hopefully—so that the sale of that property post-retirement can provide a comfortable nest egg.

- Insurance is purchased via healthcare "exchanges" or open marketplaces where users can compare plans and premiums.

By the way, you are considered covered if you have Medicare, Medicaid, CHIP, a job-based insurance plan (which you may have no longer if you are going the self-employed route), any plan you have already bought yourself, COBRA, retiree coverage, TRICARE, VA health coverage, or some other kind of health insurance. You may be able to get reduced premiums or tax subsidies to help defray some of the cost, but chances are if you are launching or have a home business, you may not qualify, as this assistance is really designed for lower-income individuals and families.

Health care exchange sign-up went live on October 1, 2013. Each state operates its own exchanges, with some opting to have the Federal government handle the exchanges, so it's difficult to provide comprehensive information for everyone (be sure to consult your insurance company or other resource for the most up-to-date information). Some states are also handling the rollout better than others. New York State, for example, has done an excellent job thus far. Not everyone has had the same experience, however. Our advice is to start at healthcare.gov and go from there.

> **In Our Experience: Plan for Premium Increases**
>
> In your cost planning, also account for annual increases in health-insurance premiums. In the fourteen years that Richard has been self-employed, there has been no year in which his health insurance premium didn't increase by less than ten percent—even post-ACA.

If you are healthy and in your twenties, you may be fairly blasé about purchasing health insurance. But as you get older, and especially if you have a family, health insurance becomes an increasingly important concern.

The best of all worlds may very well be a spouse who has a full-time job with an employer-sponsored health plan. Often these plans will also cover spouses and even families ("dependents"). The only drawback to this kind of arrangement is if the spouse loses his or her job.

Don't Go Uninsured

Even if you are young, healthy, and single, launching a business without any kind of health insurance is a big gamble. It's true that as of 2014 you were required to purchase health insurance, but even so there are some who may find it more cost effective to just pay the penalty ($95 per adult, $47.50 per child, or one percent of your income, whichever is higher, and the fee will increase every year.) If you choose to eat this penalty—likely because you are young and/or have no chronic health issues—there is always the possibility of an accident or injury that can result not only in potentially hundreds of thousands of dollars in medical bills but may also keep you from working at your fullest potential—further limiting your ability to pay your medical bills. If you only need health insurance in the case of something unforeseen, look into plans that have smaller premiums and higher deductibles, but understand that if you do have to use your insurance, you may end up paying more for health care than what you would have paid in premiums with a "better" plan.

There are two broad categories of health-insurance plans:

- *Individual/family plans.* You apply directly to an insurer for a plan that covers yourself or your family. Bear in mind that until all the initiatives of health-care reform kick in as of 2014, you can still be denied coverage if you have a pre-existing health condition.

- *Small business/group plan.* If you have other employees, you may find it cost-effective to set up a group plan, with the cost shared between employer and employee(s). (In some states, sole proprietors can qualify for group plans.)

There are some concessions you may have to make when switching plans or signing up for a new plan. The biggest may be your doctor, and if you have a regular doctor that you like, a plan that doesn't allow you to see him/her may be a deal-breaker. Many of the insurance plans you are likely to join will require you to use in-network physicians, and coordinate all care through a primary care physician (PCP). This is your gatekeeper, and if you get sick or suffer an injury, this physician will then refer you to in-network specialists. It can be a bit of a waste of time and a co-pay, but that's the way it goes.

Hi, Deductible

There are some common health-insurance terms you may not be familiar with, or you may be familiar with them from other types of insurance.

Premium. The fee paid to the insurance company regularly (usually quarterly or monthly) for basic membership in a health plan. If you are billed $2,000 every quarter by your health insurer or a third-party manager, that is your premium. All or some percentage of your premium may be tax-deductible. Be sure to ask your accountant.

Deductible. The amount you have to pay out-of-pocket before your insurance company will begin paying for a medical claim. So if you incur a $5,000 medical bill, and you have a $1,000 deductible, you are responsible for paying the first $1,000 of that bill. Premiums do not count toward your deductible.

Co-pay. A specific dollar amount you may be required to pay at the time that some service is performed. If a doctor's visit requires a $15 co-pay, you will be expected to pay $15 when you arrive for your appointment. Prescription drugs also feature co-pays. Sometimes, a health insurance plan will only cover some percentage of certain procedures, like sixty percent of x-rays. This means that you are responsible for forty percent of the cost of getting an x-ray.

Out-of-Pocket Expenses. Any medical costs you will pay for yourself, including deductibles, co-pays, and other fees and charges, which can be myriad. A health insurance plan may identify "maximum out-of-pocket costs"—the most you would ever have to pay yourself in the course of a year.

Some plans, especially those designed to be used in conjunction with health savings accounts, are what are known as "high-deductible" plans. Essentially, you agree to pay a higher deductible, often in exchange for a lower premium. A high-deductible plan may sound tempting, particularly if you are young and healthy, but they can be a gamble. You can agree to a deductible of $10,000 or $20,000, or even higher, but think about what that means. If you are in an accident, or are diagnosed with something dire (like cancer or some other illness), are you prepared to pay as much as—or perhaps even as *little* as— $10,000 or $20,000 on medical expenses alone in the course of a year?

Also pay attention to co-pays. Even seemingly small diagnostic procedures can result in a slew of invoices. Some experts recommend a choosing a deductible that is no higher than five percent of your gross annual income. When choosing a plan, be sure to get as much clarification as possible about what is covered, what is not covered, and how much co-pays for various procedures are.

Here are some types of insurance plans to consider:

- *Preferred Provider Organization (PPO).* This is a group of health-care providers (physicians, hospitals, and others) who have agreed to provide discounted health-care services[21] to an insurer's (or a third-party administrator's) clients. PPOs are good for individual and family plans, particularly if your preferred doctor is in their network.

- *Health Maintenance Organization (HMO).* Similar to a PPO, an HMO uses a network of health-care providers, and all services are coordinated via the primary care physician. All providers, such as specialists, labs, physical therapists, mental health practitioners, etc., must all be in-network, otherwise much higher co-pays are charged, if out-of-network practitioners are even covered at all. One advantage of HMOs is that they encourage preventive care—regular checkups, vaccinations, and other such services may be provided free or have co-pays less than visits for other purposes.

> ### Eyes and Teeth
> Not all plans cover vision or dental services. Some will cover regular eye and/or dental examinations, but nothing beyond that, like glasses/contact lenses in the case of optometry, or fillings, oral surgery, orthodontics, etc., in the case of dentistry. If you need these services to be covered, you may need to shop around.

- *Point of Service (POS).* A more flexible version of an HMO in which health care is coordinated by an in-network PCP (which is the point-of-service), who may make referrals outside the network—although the patient may pay greater co-pays and other costs out-of-pocket.

---

[21] This is really why insurance has become so necessary; hospitals and other providers have a "chargemaster," which is the master price list of every product and service the provider offers, from lab tests, to surgical gowns, to bandages. This chargemaster's prices are what an uninsured patient would be charged for these materials, which is often exponentially higher that what an insurance company would be billed.

Check Your Chamber

In the past, Chambers of Commerce have offered their members the ability to get health insurance through the Chamber's own group plan. After the implementation of the Affordable Care Act (ACA), Chambers are no longer able to do this, at least for sole proprietorships, and are funneling members through the Exchanges, which opened for business on October 1, 2013. Still, local Chambers of Commerce can be good resources for navigating the health insurance changes coming via the ACA and how they apply to small businesses and sole proprietorships.

- *Health Savings Account (HSA)-Eligible Plans.* Some health-insurance plans are designed to be used in conjunction with a "health savings account," which is a bank account that lets patients squirrel away funds—pre-tax—that are used solely for medical care in the future, particularly "catastrophic" care. It's like a retirement account, but for health-care. HSAs can accrue interest, and they roll over every year. The M.O. of a "high-deductible" health-care plan (see the sidebar on the next page) is that patients save money on premiums (which are lower than other types of health-care plans), and instead put what would have gone to the insurance company as a premium into an HSA instead. In theory. This is a good approach if you are young, healthy, and don't visit doctors except for routine checkups.

The Affordable Care Act places limits on HSAs and FSAs, and those regulations will be changing every year, at least until 2018, when the full program is expected to be in full force. Be sure to check with your insurance company and tax advisor every year. This should not be considered as "once and done."

Assess Your Insurance Needs

When shopping for plans, ask some basic questions:

- Who needs to be covered? Just yourself? Yourself and a spouse? Dependents? If others will need coverage, does everyone need to be on the same plan, or would covering different family members with their own separate plans make more sense in the long run?

- How much do you—i.e., your business—have in the bank? This is important for determining how large a deductible you are comfortable with. You may be young and healthy, but accidents can happen at any time.

- Do you have any pre-existing medical conditions? While you can no longer be denied coverage, account for the likely expenses related to your condition, such as routine lab tests, prescription medications, and other supplies and services.

- Add up your total medical expenses—and those of others who will need to be covered—to determine what you are likely going to spend in the future. Of course, if your medical expenses were under $100 last year, but this year you are joining an extreme sports league, your needs may end up changing.

Constant Changes

Health insurance options are constantly changing and, unfortunately, are subject to political forces. It's therefore very important to stay ahead on top of this issue, especially if you are just entering the home office environment. If there's anything that can surprise people who leave jobs and then have to go on their own, it's an uncontrollable fixed cost that can't really be managed by determining how much you will use. A good accountant, and a good insurance agent, can make sure that you get the right subsidy....*and* how to make sure you don't lose it. You could conceivably work for "nothing," get a full subsidy for insurance, and be packing money away into IRAs and HSAs and becoming wealthy in the process. Also, if you have a partner whose insurance is covered and you are part of that policy, you have a distinct advantage over other home office businesses who are not in that situation. That's all the more reason to maximize IRA and health-care contributions because the joint tax return will be at a higher income tax rate. Take advantage of every deduction for tax-deferred investments. Again, check with your accountant, because if you are covered by another person's policy, you may not be able to open an HSA. But it's a great long-term investment if you can because it will compound tax-free for a long period of time and can be a great buffer if the insurance status of the covered partner changes.

Expect to review your health care plan annually, particularly given that the Affordable Care Act can change from year-to-year, but especially because premiums go up every year. New options are always appearing, and you may have gleaned some experience in the first year of a particular plan and need one with different types of coverage. (One year Richard experimented with a high-deductible plan. He won't do that again!) You may also have had some life changes that will impact your health insurance needs. You may have had a change in marital status or had children. Your grown children may have moved out and secured their own health insurance coverage. You may have had a change in health status; were you diagnosed with an illness or, on the brighter side, did you lose a lot of weight and got fit and healthier?

These are all things that you should review annually.

Other Types of Insurance

Health insurance is not the only type of insurance that is available to you as a business, although it may be the most significant. Depending upon the business you are in, you may want other types of insurance, such as disability (if you suffer an injury or illness that prevents you from working, can your business still function?), property insurance (this may be covered by your homeowners policy), professional/specialty liability (if you are sued for negligence or other error in the course of providing a product or service), commercial vehicle insurance, life insurance, and more. There is even a product called "umbrella insurance," which is a type of liability insurance that kicks in should any losses exceed what is covered by any other primary policy. When you meet with your business attorney, be sure to ask what type of insurance, if any, s/he would recommend for your specific home business.

Moving Forward

In this chapter we looked at the nuts and bolts of setting up the business, dealing with accounting, taxes, and insurance. It is impossible to address every potential topic of every potential home business, but we hope we have given you some helpful pointers and a set of the right questions to ask.

The final chapter will provide a timeline/to-do list that presents all the "action items" we have identified in this book in more or less the order you should address them.

To Do:

❑ Meet with a business attorney to discuss your proposed business and any potential snafus that may arise.

❑ Meet with an accountant and discuss projected revenue (as best you can project it) and a strategy for estimating your taxes.

❑ Decide whether your business is best set up as a sole proprietorship, an S corporation, or a limited liability company (LLC).

❑ Set up a business bank account.

❑ Apply for a credit card you will only use for business expenses.

❑ Investigate and purchase the appropriate software for your business bookkeeping. Don't be afraid to buy an accompanying *Quicken for Dummies* book if learning software isn't easy for you.

❑ Assess your health insurance needs and compare plans. Apply for the plan that looks like it will best suit your needs.

❑ And while you're at it, why not schedule a physical as soon as you have chosen a primary care physician. You want to make sure that you don't have any undiscovered health problems that will impede your ability to launch your business.

❑ Decide—with your business attorney—if you require any other type of insurance, like liability insurance.

CHAPTER

The Home Office Checklist

"That's what college is for—getting as many bad decisions as possible out of the way before you're forced into the real world. I keep a checklist of 'em on the wall in my room."

—Jeph Jacques, cartoonist

"The brain is a wonderful organ. It starts working the moment you get up in the morning and does not stop until you get into the office."

—Robert Frost, poet

This chapter will provide the action items from the previous seven chapters in more or less the order in which they should be done, with a reference to the original chapter if you need more information.

❏ Ask yourself, and answer honestly: "Why do you want to work at home?" (*Chapter 1*)

❏ Determine if you have adequate money in savings to start your business or if you need to take out a small business loan. And do you have enough in savings to tide you over until your business becomes sustainable? (*Take a Deep Breath...*)

❏ Meet with a business attorney to discuss your proposed business and any potential snafus that may arise. (*Chapter 7*)

❏ Meet with an accountant. Discuss projected revenue—as best you can project it—and a strategy for estimating your taxes. (*Chapter 7*)

❏ Decide whether your business is best set up as a sole proprietorship, an S corporation, or a limited liability company (LLC). (*Chapter 7*)

❏ Set up a business bank account. (*Chapter 7*)

❏ Apply for a credit card you will only use for business expenses. (*Chapter 7*)

❏ Assess your health insurance needs and compare plans. Apply for the plan that looks like it will best suit your needs. You may have already done this when you signed up for the Affordable Care Act health exchange. (*Chapter 7*)

❏ Schedule a physical as soon as you have chosen a primary care physician. (*Chapter 7*)

❏ Decide—with your business attorney—if you require any other type of insurance, like liability insurance. (*Chapter 7*)

❏ Check the Small Business Administration website and review the summary of zoning laws and see if any of the issues raised affect your home business. Also discuss this with your business attorney. (*Chapter 2*)

❏ Consult the bylaws of any homeowners, condo associations, co-op boards, etc., you may be a member of to ensure that you are not risking violation by setting up your home business. (*Chapter 2*)

❏ Review the Small Business Administration's section on permits and licenses and make sure you get the correct paperwork. (*Chapter 2*)

❏ Identify the optimal location in your home for your office. Be sure to clearly define the boundaries of the office space. (*Chapter 2*)

❏ Make sure your chosen office location gets strong cellphone and wireless network signals. (*Chapter 2*)

❏ Go shopping! Make a list of the furniture, hardware, and software you will need for your home office, and start picking it out. Check out Craigslist or other classified advertising for used office furniture, or search online at, say, IKEA. (*Chapter 3*)

❏ Investigate and purchase the appropriate software for your business bookkeeping. Don't be afraid to buy an accompanying *Quicken for Dummies* book if learning software isn't easy for you. (*Chapter 7*)

❏ Experiment with cloud storage or other cloud-based services and software. Get familiar with how they work, if you have not already. (*Chapter 3*)

❏ Think about the connectivity trinity: mail, phone, and Internet. Identify what you want your business mailing address, phone number, and e-mail address to be. Do you want to share it with your residential service? (*Chapter 3*)

❏ Compare mailbox rates at the Post Office and a third-party location, like The UPS Store. Consider what types of mail and packages you may be receiving. If you'll be receiving FedEx or UPS packages, a P.O. box may be impractical. (*Chapter 3*)

❏ Identify the various collateral materials you'll need. Business cards? Letterhead? Envelopes/mailing labels? (*Chapter 6*)

❑ Get to work developing your company website, either by doing it yourself or hiring a web designer. Make sure you purchase a good domain name for your business. (*Chapter 6*)

❑ Determine what time(s) of day are your most productive. Find out when you at your most alert and focused, and when you are your most sluggish. To the best of your ability, given your specific household circumstances, set these as your office hours. (*Chapter 4*)

❑ Tell the other members of your household what these hours are, and that you should not be interrupted—unless it's an emergency—during those times. (*Chapter 4*)

❑ Make sure you have a "do not disturb" sign at the ready should something come up that requires you to enter "Fortress of Solitude" mode. (*Chapter 4*)

❑ If it is necessary, communicate your work schedule to colleagues or collaborators. It might be best to phrase this as "best times to reach me" rather than "this is when I am working." (*Chapter 4*)

❑ Identify the means by which you will need to stay in contact with colleagues, coworkers, or clients. AIM? Skype? iChat? A proprietary corporate messaging system? (*Chapter 5*)

❑ Experiment with the software and know how to tell potential messagers that you are receptive—or not—to communicating. (*Chapter 5*)

❑ Explore options to set up tele- or videoconferences, if needed. (*Chapter 5*)

❑ Write and craft your elevator speech. Practice it on friends, family, or colleagues. Revise, revise, revise, and practice, practice, practice. (*Chapter 5*)

❑ Identify two or three in-person networking events over the course of the next month and develop some realistic expectations of what you want to get out of these events. Then, of course, go to them. (*Chapter 5*)

❑ Think about a marketing plan. Whom are you trying to reach, and what would likely be the best way of reaching them? (*Chapter 6*)

❑ Become active in the "Big Three" social media—Facebook, LinkedIn, and Twitter. Create and refine a good profile, and develop a schedule for posting regular updates and engaging in other activities. (*Chapter 6*)

❑ Consider taking advantage of some of LinkedIn's new services, such as Slideshare or Pulse, or services like branded.me that uses Linked In profiles as the basis of personal websites. (*Chapter 6*)

❑ Review our list of media channels. Identify five or six channels you would be comfortable implementing immediately and another five or six that you would want to implement, but would require more money, time, and/or expertise than you possess. (*Chapter 6*)

❑ Decide what your metrics for success will be—based on realistic expectations. What results in what time period would you consider a success vs. a failure? And if a failure occurs, be honest about what the problems might have been. Too little activity on your own part? The wrong kind of activity? Before abandoning an idea completely, see if, with a little retooling or extra effort, it could be made to pay off. (*Chapter 6*)

CHAPTER

Habits to Pick Up— And Habits to Break

"My problem lies in reconciling my gross habits with my net income."
—Errol Flynn, movie actor

"Good habits result from resisting temptation."
—Ancient Proverb

As you have no doubt surmised throughout this book, working from home and running a home business requires considerable discipline. And a large part of developing that discipline is picking up good habits and breaking bad ones. We all have both, and they can mean the difference between success and failure. So in this final chapter, we list a few good habits you should get into—and some bad ones you should break. Do an honest self-assessment and identify which habits to keep and which ones to break. Self-assessment tools like the Greatest Strengths Report (see page 208) can also be a helpful guide to identifying where you excel and where you need some work.

Habits to Pick Up

❑ Keep a regular work schedule—whatever those hours may be.

❑ Tell spouses, children, or other cohabitants not to disturb you at certain times of the working day—your "office hours." Also be sure to set up times when you will always be available.

❑ Ensure that phone calls and video conferences are free from distracting background noise or activity—or at least as free as you can make it.

❑ Develop the ability to "switch off" and not work during your dedicated downtime.

❑ File physical materials such as documents, receipts, statements, etc., in a timely and effective fashion. Don't let it pile up on your desk or in a drawer.

❑ Diligently name and store computer files in a way that will allow you to find them again in the future—perhaps even long after you have forgotten about them.

❑ Work in the cloud.

❑ Enter all business expenses into your chosen accounting system in a timely manner. Save receipts (either physically or digitally) so that you can easily access them and supply to your accountant.

❏ Use only your dedicated credit card and bank account for business expenses.

❏ Be able to talk with energy and enthusiasm (and no false modesty) about your business.

❏ Pick a social media strategy and diligently and persistently post updates and otherwise remain active and visible.

❏ Attend in-person networking events at least once a month.

❏ Have business cards on hand at all times. Even if you're just going to the supermarket, you never know whom you may run into.

❏ Always dress better than the people you are meeting. Although it's not necessary for you to deliver a presentation in a tuxedo or a ball gown, a basic business suit and understated accessories always convey professionalism.

Habits to Break

❏ Dropping everything to answer the phone—especially the cellphone—or read an incoming e-mail.

❏ Indulging spouses, children, or other cohabitants whenever they see fit to disturb you.

❏ Throwing all papers and other physical materials into a single drawer or folder.

❏ Naming computer files randomly and vaguely. If your Excel files are all named "Book1.xlsx," you're already in trouble.

❏ Waiting until you have a serious problem to find a computer repair or tech support expert.

❏ Relying too heavily on new technology. How many times has someone brought a tablet or a smartphone to a business meeting to take notes or present ideas—rather than a more reliable medium, like a pen and paper—and been flummoxed when there were technical problems? Having to admit that "this isn't working correctly" reflects badly on your business.

❏ Charging everything to the business, even if it is a personal expense. If the IRS finds this in an audit, it only makes them want to probe deeper. If they see a distinct separation, they move on to other things.

Good Habits I Should Pick Up...

_____

_____

_____

_____

_____

Bad Habits I Should Break...

_____

_____

_____

_____

_____

CHAPTER **10**

The Home Office That Works Web Links

In this book, we have used a URL-shortening service to keep web addresses in the text to a reasonable length. However, shortened links sometimes expire, so in this appendix we have included the original long links as well as QR codes in case you dislike typing URLs as much as we do. If you have a QR code reader on your mobile device, simply scan the code and you'll be taken to the appropriate site. Or you can go to www.homeofficethatworks.com and click the live links.

Chapter 2

Page 18: SBA's "Home-Based Zoning Laws"
http://www.sba.gov/content/zoning-laws-home-based-businesses

Page 18: NFIB Home-based business tips
http://www.nfib.com/business-resources/start-a-business/home-based-business/

Page 19: SBA's "Permit Me"
http://www.sba.gov/licenses-and-permits

Page 30: Office pods
http://www.businesspundit.com/15-incredible-outdoor-office-pods/

Page 37: *Richmond Times-Dispatch* story on coworking spaces
http://www.richmond.com/business/local/article_a295b084-7119-5c67-94df-87655d1e56c9.html

Chapter 3

Page 48: *PC World* cloud storage reviews
http://www.pcworld.com/article/2975913/home-players/western-digital-my-cloud-update-adds-phone-backup-shared-albums-with-friends.html

Page 56: Footnote reference to *Wall Street Journal* "ditch your PC" article
http://online.wsj.com/articles/you-can-ditch-your-pc-now-1415570187

Chapter 4

Page 68: Footnote reference to ABC story about the genetic basis for morning and night persons
http://abcnews.go.com/blogs/health/2011/11/28/scientists-id-morning-person-gene/

Chapter 5

Page 96: Wikipedia list of trade associations
http://en.wikipedia.org/wiki/List_of_industry_trade_groups_in_the_United_States

Chapter 6

Page 107: Footnote reference to *"Does a Plumber Need a Web Site?"*
http://www.lulu.com/shop/joseph-webb/does-a-plumber-need-a-web-site/paperback/product-18648667.html

Page 123: Every Door Direct Mail
https://www.usps.com/business/every-door-direct-mail.htm

Page 124: Footnote reference to how to record a podcast
http://www.brendoman.com/index.php/2012/05/31/how-to-record-a-podcast

Page 128: "The Missing Link" podcast
http://rainmaker.fm/series/link/

Page 130: Footnote reference to LinkedIn resources
http://www.powerformula.net/free-resources-for-learning-linkedin

Page 131: Setting up a YouTube channel
http://www.youtube.com/watch?v=gQ9JXbK5quU

Chapter 7

Page 141:

Footnote reference to IRS information on husband-and-wife businesses
http://www.irs.gov/Businesses/Small-Businesses-&-Self-Employed/Husband-and-Wife-Business

Footnote reference to IRS information on sole proprietorships
http://www.irs.gov/Businesses/Small-Businesses-&-Self-Employed/Sole-Proprietorships

Footnote reference to IRS information on partnerships
http://www.irs.gov/Businesses/Small-Businesses-&-Self-Employed/Partnerships

Page 142:

Footnote reference to IRS information on corporations and C corporations
http://www.irs.gov/Businesses/Small-Businesses-&-Self-Employed/Corporations

Footnote reference to IRS information on S corporations
http://www.irs.gov/Businesses/Small-Businesses-&-Self-Employed/S-Corporations

Page 143:

Footnote reference to IRS information on Limited
Liability Companies
http://www.irs.gov/Businesses/Small-Businesses-&-Self-
Employed/Limited-Liability-Company-LLC

Page 147:

Accounting software reviews
http://accounting-software-review.toptenreviews.com/

Footnote reference to Quicken/QuickBooks
comparison
http://www.redlig.com/quick_compare.shtml

Page 157:

Footnote reference to IRS information about the
home office deduction
http://www.irs.gov/Businesses/Small-Businesses-&-Self-
Employed/Home-Office-Deduction

Appendix

Page 196: Footnote reference to *New York Times*
story about why we hate work
http://www.nytimes.com/2014/06/01/opinion/sunday/
why-you-hate-work.html.

Page 197: Footnote reference to CNN story about
misuse of 911
http://money.cnn.com/2014/08/04/news/companies/
facebook-outage-911/

Page 198: Footnote reference to The Home Office That
Works Blog post about companies that lease out their
space to teleworkers
http://homeofficethatworks.com/blog/your-home-office-
away-from-home/

...Okay, You Can Exhale Now

A lot of information has been presented in the preceding chapters. We hope we haven't needlessly frightened anyone or given you a case of informational indigestion. The goal has been for you to use this book as a general plan of action for putting together a home office and running a home-based business. Do we expect everyone (or anyone) to follow every single one of the steps we have outlined? Of course not. And, in fact, *we* haven't! We learned a lot of what we've presented in this book by trial and error over the years. You will have your share of mistakes as you experience working at home. No one ever gets it right the first time—and what fun would it be if we did? We learn from our mistakes, more so than from our successes, and it has been our intent to share some of what we have learned in the decades that we have been working from home.

What we do want to stress, however, is that you shouldn't become so obsessive about getting all the administrative details perfect that you neglect the tasks that comprise your actual business. It's entirely possible that, like many of us, you were abruptly thrust into your home office with a major project and a tight deadline. So you may not actually have the luxury of time and or funds to set up a full-featured office, or make decisions about sole proprietorships and S corporations, or evaluate accounting software, at least not right away. And that's okay. Do what you need to do to get the business going. Just remember to return to these other items sooner rather than later; April 15 is also a deadline. It's best not to be scrambling at the last minute—and it's best not to let surprises disrupt the normal flow of regular work. It's nice to have downtime once in a while, but the goal is to always be working on *some* kind of project, and taking time away from that to handle something unforeseen may be disruptive.

We wish you the best of success in your new endeavor.

APPENDIX

Making the Home Office Work for Teleworkers and Managers

This book is intended to be a comprehensive guidebook to running and working from a home office, whether you are operating a home-based business or teleworking to a full-time job. Either way, the intended readers are the teleworking employees themselves.

But what about their employers?

For this 2016 revision, we added this Appendix to offer some advice and guidance for those who hire and manage teleworkers.

Since the first edition of this book, we have forged a relationship with Peak Focus, an administrator of the Harrison Assessment, a highly effective and widely respected tool for evaluating potential employees' preferences, motivations and behavioral traits, to assess those traits that will make a potential employee a successful teleworker.

We discuss the Harrison Assessment in the context of teleworkers in detail later in this Appendix.

The Modern Teleworker

Teleworking has many advantages for both employer and employee alike. However, the traditional employee screening and hiring process may not be adequate for gauging who will be a productive teleworker, and who will become a problem.

An Employee Without an Office

A publishing company for which Richard freelances closed its Long Island office at the end of 2014, and the full-time employees were directed to work from home—or move to the main office in Wisconsin.

More and more companies are allowing—and sometimes mandating—their employees work at home, either part- or full-time. Many companies now recruit for full-time telecommuting positions as part of their normal staffing plans.

In Chapter 1, we identify the advantages of telecommuting can from the employee's standpoint, which include things like:

- the re-claiming of commuting time into work and family time
- more flexible time to spend with family, especially children
- avoidance of meetings, "office politics," and other workplace distractions
- more productive work time
- the potential ability to live where one wants, improving quality of life

There are several advantages from the employer's standpoint, as well, such as:

- less need for office space
- potentially less need for office equipment like computers, peripherals, and other resources
- better employee morale
- potentially more productive employees

While there are advantages to having employees telecommute, there are potential disadvantages from both the employee's and employer's standpoints.

For the employee, as we say in Chapter 1, these can include:

- managing distractions, like family, pets, home maintenance, etc.
- the logistics and expense of setting up a home office, even despite guidance and contribution by the employer
- lack of office collaboration, camaraderie, and a change to business culture
- no distinction between "home" and "work," leading to burnout

For the employer...well, the disadvantages really can be boiled down to just one basic concern:

- is the employee actually working?

FLIRTING WITH DISASTER

Consider some of these teleworking "fails":

- "Harold" is a middle-aged teleworker. It seems impossible to get him on the phone and takes hours to respond to e-mail because it seems there is always something to do around the house. The lawn always needs mowing, the yard raking, the driveway snow-shoveled—you name it. And it's only when these items are attended to that he returns to work. You can work at night, but yardwork has to be done in the daytime.

- "Ellen" is a mother of pre-school-age children and is allowed to work from home. Her productivity is negatively impacted by constantly being distracted by the needs of her children. Conference calls are inevitably interrupted by the din of screaming and crying.[1]

- "Jack" is a young, twentysomething guy who is allowed to work from home. His productivity has been falling. Unbeknownst to his employer, Jack has taken to going "out on the town" several nights during the week and is often—shall we say—under the weather until late morning or early afternoon. Token answering of email or participation in virtual meetings gives the illusion that he is working, but when his actual productivity is taken into account, it's clear there is a problem.

- "Janice" is a social person. When she had a full-time in-office job, she was often reprimanded for her personal calls, or for updating her Facebook status at her desk. Now, allowed to work from home, she has unfettered access to all forms of personal social interaction—and her work is less than it was in the office.

---

[1] A colleague of ours related a story that she was on an audio-only conference call and she determined that one of the women on the call was breastfeeding. Our colleague had to call the nursing mother and point this out, just in case others realized it, indicating she was doing something other than working.

- "Dave" just doesn't like to work. Left to his own devices, he'll do the bare minimum that is required of him, but is more inclined to lie on the couch and watch TV than work to his fullest.

If you have been in a managerial position for any length of time, none of these "disaster scenarios" will be much of a surprise to you—and you probably have countless others we could have included. At the same time, working in an office full-time isn't always a complete solution; in-office workers can easily be distracted by non-essential tasks, make personal calls/social media updates on company time, take three-hour lunch breaks, and otherwise work unproductively. They can also lose time waiting in meetings. But in an office environment, these things can be more closely monitored by both employee and manager and corrected. When the employee is trusted to work at home, that's largely what it is: a matter of trust. If productivity suffers in a noticeable and quantifiable way, the behavior can be corrected, but it may be too late. A deadline may have been missed, a client may have been lost, or there was some other negative impact to the company as a whole.

AVERTING DISASTER

One way of avoiding any of the teleworker disasters cited above is to hire employees who have personal traits that support productive telework. The Harrison Assessment tools can be part of that process (described below).

Once you have hired someone and allowed them to work from home, it seems like it's a big gamble to give them that freedom. Who's to say they won't slack off?

That's the wrong way to think about teleworkers, or employees in general. There really is no evidence to suggest—much less prove— that a teleworking employee is any less productive than a non-teleworking employee.

We believe that most people—or at least most people who are likely to be in a position where teleworking is an option—want to work, and want to do a good job. In fact, ask anyone what they hate most about their jobs, they'll probably tell you (after "they don't pay me enough") things like "no time for creative or strategic thinking," "inability to focus on one thing at a time," "no great meaning or significance," "inability to balance work and home life," and so on.[2] They may also identify things like "office politics," "my boss," and "no sense of autonomy." They might say "the time lost when I'm commuting to the office."

Of course, allowing employees to work at home won't solve all those problems, but it does give employees a sense of autonomy, and the sense that the company trusts them with a greater degree of responsibility than if they were being watched all the time. People like to be trusted, and unless there is some specific reason to think that trust isn't warranted, giving the employee the benefit of the doubt can go a long way toward instilling the drive on the part of the employee to want to do a good job.

That said, the initial few weeks of teleworking will likely be a little rocky, as the teleworker adjusts to the new office setting and settles into a routine. As we point out in Chapter 4, setting up the office, working out a schedule, communicating it to other family members, and "troubleshooting" the whole process can take some time. Obviously, productive work needs to get done during this period, but managers should understand that it can take some time to get into a routine.

PRODUCTIVE WORK DOESN'T ONLY HAPPEN AT A DESK

There is a tendency to want teleworkers—or any workers—to always be at their desks, as that seems like it is the best indication that someone is working. However, depending on the nature of the work, sometimes one can be productive and be nowhere near a desk. If it's some kind of creative work, sometimes it is easier to focus while taking a walk or going for a run. Sometimes—as we point out in the discussion of the "Fortress of Solitude"—it's necessary

---

[2] Tony Schwartz and Christine Porath, "Why You Hate Work," *New York Times*, May 30, 2014, http://nyti.ms/1oX2v1W.

to "go dark" and turn off phones, e-mail, and instant messaging. It's tempting to say "I'm the boss!" and insist on always having access to a teleworker, but that may not be realistic and can cause friction.

However, both telemanager and teleworker need to work out a system for emergency situations. The teleworker may be in the Fortress of Solitude mode[3]—but what happens when there is an emergency that requires getting touch ASAP? In Chapter 4, we mention using special e-mail addresses, Skype or IM user names, or even super-secret phone numbers that are to be used in case of emergency. And the manager should recognize that this contact method should be used only in an emergency, not for random "checking up."[4]

WHEN THERE IS A PROBLEM

When an employee first begins teleworking, we would recommend a two- to three-week grace period to work all the bugs out of the home office system. If, after that grace period is up, productivity remains low, if tasks or projects are not getting done, if phone calls or e-mails are not being returned in a timely manner, or if anything affecting the business is suffering, then perhaps there is a more serious problem with the arrangement. The solution is not immediate dismissal, but a firm but friendly conversation with the employee. "Is there a problem? How can the problem be solved?" It may very well be more of a disruption to the business to fire and replace an employee than to try to remedy the situation. It may very well be the case that a particular employee is not temperamentally suited to teleworking—and, in fact, may just not like it. That's perfectly fine. No one has to.

If that is the case, you and the employee should explore options. Can s/he go back to working in the company office? Maybe

---

[3] In Chapter 4, we recommend that when home office workers need to focus with laser-like precision on a task at hand to, if possible, turn off the phone, e-mail, etc., and enter what we referred to as "Fortress of Solitude" mode *à la* Superman.
[4] Even 911, the quintessential emergency number, can be misused. Yes, people have called 911 when Facebook has gone down (http://cnnmon.ie/1s8q8IN).

part-time teleworking—say, two or three days a week—would be a compromise. If there is no main office, would there be a way for two or more geographically proximate employees could work together, at least part of the time? Sometimes just having a coworker nearby can reduce or eliminate the sense of isolation that working from home can cause.

If there really is no choice—the office has been shut down and all its employees are teleworkers—how can you work with an employee to improve the situation? Find out what it is about working from home that is the issue. Would finding some sort of exterior working arrangement—at least part of the time—be a better option? Last year, we wrote on The Home Office That Works blog about companies that lease out their space—at least part-time—to teleworkers.[5] Would that be an option—logistically or financially?

Teleworker problems may not be completely insoluble and don't have to end in termination. Unfortunately, that may be required, but be sure you haven't explored all the other possible solutions before you reach for the pink slip.

Hire With Teleworking in Mind: Harrison Assessments

The best way to avoid potential problems with teleworkers is to hire employees who are already cut out for teleworking. It comes down to hiring the "right" people.

Now, hiring the "right" employee, one who has not only the skills for a particular job, but also those behavioral traits that make them a good employee, has always been a challenge for employers. Even people who seem to have great resumés and stellar references, and ace a job interview, can turn into disasters once they're hired. And, conversely, it's not unheard of that the least appealing job candidates end up being the best employees. In general, you just never know.

---

[5] "The Home Office Away From Home," http://bit.ly/1vFLBVE.

Hiring employees in general is tough enough, but the traits that make a good teleworker add a new layer of complexity to that challenge. How does an employer assess these individuals during the hiring process? How can companies determine in advance who in their current staff will be able to work productively from home, and who will fall into one of the disaster scenarios cited above?

Enter Harrison Assessments.

We worked with Peak Focus, a licensed distributor of the Harrison Assessments, to tailor an Assessment to evaluate those traits that make a good—or bad—teleworker.

Some of this is going to sound a little like an infomercial, but we'll try to keep that under control.

OVERVIEW OF HARRISON ASSESSMENTS

The Harrison Assessment process was founded in 1990 by Dan Harrison, Ph.D., whose background in such diverse disciplines as mathematics, personality theory, counseling psychology, and organizational psychology, led him to develop a unique employee assessment methodology. The resulting Harrison Assessment tools help organizations worldwide hire, develop, promote, and retain top talent. Harrison Assessments is fully customizable, and its job analysis and integrated employee assessment tools and technologies are pretty accurate in ensuring a good job fit, and do a pretty good job of predicting job success—from entry level all the way up to top executive management. Harrison Assessments tools have become the most trusted and accurate employee assessment tools in the industry.[6]

The Harrison test authentication methods include three psychological methodologies and one technological mechanism.[7] Re-

---

[6] One of the M.O.s behind Harrison Assessments is to prevent employees and employers from "cheating," and thus deliver valid results. Many individuals—as many as 10% by some estimates—attempt to cheat or skew behavioral assessment tests. Even HR professionals know how to "game" such tests. However, the authentication methods used by Harrison Assessments makes it virtually impossible for candidates or HR professionals to scam the Assessment.

[7] We could tell you what those mechanisms are, but then we'd have to kill you. We don't think that's a healthy author–reader relationship.

search has found that candidates who *did* pass the assessment and were subsequently hired showed a strong positive correlation with job performance.

HARRISON ASSESSMENTS METHODOLOGY—AVOIDING BARTLEBYS

In Herman Melville's classic short story "Bartleby the Scrivener," the titular scribe works for a high-powered Wall Street law firm and turns out high-quality work. However, over the course of the story, the quality and quantity of his work declines, and when asked to perform certain tasks, he replies with what becomes his stock line: "I would prefer not to." By the end of the story, the number of things that Bartleby would prefer not to do has increased exponentially.[8]

A good employee-job fit, therefore, is one in which the job consists of things that he or she would, in fact, prefer to do.

It should come as no surprise that people who enjoy their work do well at their jobs. Obviously, no one is going to like every single aspect of their jobs; that's just not realistic. But twenty years worth of research has found that employees who enjoy at least seventy-five percent of their job are three times more likely to succeed than employees who like only twenty-fve percent of their job. The Harrison Assessments methodology is based on examining what it is that a job candidate in fact likes doing, and the extent to which they take satisfaction in doing certain types of tasks. The goal is to determine how much satisfaction that candidate will take in the job, and thus how well they will perform in it.

Harrison Assessments look at three areas:

- the extent to which the *tasks an individual prefers doing* match the tasks that the job comprises

- the extent to which the *things an individual is interested in* match the things the job comprises

- the extent to which an individual's *preferred work environ-*

---

[8] See http://en.wikipedia.org/wiki/Bartleby,_the_Scrivener. Spoiler alert: he eventually starves to death because he preferred not to eat.

ment matches that of the job

Harrison Assessments gauge how satisfied a potential employee will be in a given job, which corresponds to how well they will perform that job. And good performance leads to acknowledgment and reward, boosting self-esteem, and in turn increasing satisfaction. This creates an important feedback loop that ensures continually improved performance and satisfaction—and a situation that is win-win for both employee and employer.

ANALYZING KEY TRAITS

Harrison Assessments measure up to 175 traits, including motivations, personality traits, interests, work values, and work preferences. These traits are evaluated using what is called the Smart-Questionnaire, which requires the applicant to rank a series of self-descriptive sentences in order. The various traits are then scored based on those responses. Naturally, each job or behavioral competency will require a different set and combination of traits, which is why Harrison Assessments are customizable. The methodology is tweaked based on which traits are best suited for a particular job or behavioral competency.

In addition to the SmartQuestionnaire, Harrison Assessments also use what is called Paradox Technology, which looks at the way the individual selected the various items on the SmartQuestionnaire and determines what the individual's *traits to avoid* are, and identifies behavioral issues that could negatively affect job performance, job fit and competencies.

As we said, all jobs require a unique set of traits and competencies, and this is also true for teleworkers. So we worked with Peak Focus to develop a set of traits and a methodology that will allow companies to screen potential teleworkers in advance, avoiding the various teleworking disasters cited earlier.

USING HARRISON ASSESSMENTS IN THE SCREENING PROCESS

The assessment process is fairly straightforward. The job applicant takes an online test, and our software algorithms and analysts go to work analyzing the responses to that test. A report is generated that ranks the various traits according to how each trait is likely to affect job performance, both in general and as a teleworker.

How to Apply the Assessment

Ultimately, the assessment is used to evaluate behavioral competency. For our purposes, we can define "competency" as an attribute, knowledge, skill, ability, or other characteristic that contributes to successful job performance. Behavioral competencies are observable and measurable behaviors, knowledge, skills, abilities, and other characteristics that contribute to individual success in an organization. Telecommuting jobs require a wide range of "competencies" depending on the specific requirements of the particular job, but they also require certain basic behavioral competencies in order for the employee to function effectively as a teleworker. We have identified the basic competencies for successful corporate telecommuters.

Harrison Assessments for Teleworkers is an online test that takes about twenty to thirty minutes for an applicant to complete. It asks the assessee to rank several statements about different types of tasks or work situations, in the order in which s/he agrees with those statements. Some examples are:

"I enjoy working with my hands."

"I would enjoy working with computers."

"I enjoy analyzing problems and decisions."

"I enjoy meeting and mixing with many new people."

"I enjoy being in a leadership role."

"I am able to deal with conflict effectively."

And so forth. Once the results are submitted, they are analyzed and a report is generated.

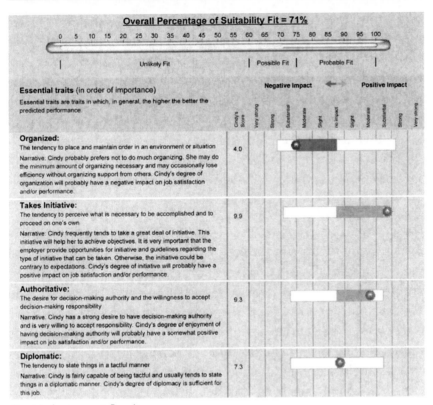

Sample Assessment Results

How to Interpret the Results

Each report ranks a variety of "essential traits" (helpful, persistent, etc.), "desirable traits" (comfort with technology, optimistic, analytical, etc.), and "traits to avoid" (blunt, defensive, dominating, etc.), ranking them on a scale from "highest negative impact" to "highest positive impact."

The scale is also color coded to show whether a given trait will have a positive (green), neutral (yellow), or negative (red) impact on the employee's performance. In the portion of a sample assessment illustrated above, although it is in black-and-white the negative traits extend to the left, positive ones to the right. We can see that the candidate is not very organized, which will have a substantial negative impact on this candidate's performance as a telework-

205

er. On the other hand, the candidate ranked very high on "takes initiative," which will have a substantial positive impact on their ability to perform as a teleworker. The candidate is fairly "authoritative"—or has a higher-than-average desire for decision-making authority—which will have a slight to moderate positive impact on her ability to perform as a teleworker. In terms of the degree to which this applicant is "diplomatic"—or can state things tactfully—the score indicates that this candidate's diplomatic skills will have no impact on her ability to function as a teleworker.

Putting the Results In Context

The customized Harrison Assessment is a highly useful tool for evaluating potential employees, but it works best as one piece of a larger puzzle. *The Home Office That Works!* authors will help put the quantitative results of Harrison Assessments into context, and help evaluate one candidate in comparison to another. Another place where we can help is in coaching potential employees. As employers evaluate resumés and references, they may find that one particular candidate has the exact skills and previous experience that would be ideal for a position—but Harrison Assessments result suggest that the candidate may not be 100% ideal as a teleworker. We can work with employers to groom otherwise perfect candidates into ideal teleworkers.[9] Using *The Home Office That Works!* as the basic text, we can work with employers to go "beyond the Assessment" and help teleworking-averse employees improve those areas that the Assessment has found lacking.

What Are Your Greatest Strengths?

In addition to employers and current employees, readers of this book may also be actively—or may find themselves—applying for a teleworking position. If you are a prospective teleworking employee, while we can't promise that indicating on your resumé

---

[9] You've heard perhaps of "software as a service" or "marketing as a service"? Think of this as "book authorship as a service"!

that you've read this book will help your prospects any[10], taking the Harrison Assessment for Teleworkers may. A link to Harrison Assessments tailored for teleworkers can be found on *The Home Office That Works!* website at www.homeofficethatworks.com.

Our friends at Peak Focus also have a stripped down assessment called the *Greatest Strengths Report*, which is an online assessment that will not only identify what those strengths are (sometimes we ourselves don't even know!), let you focus on what you're good at, and let you share the results with prospective employers and on social media like LinkedIn. It only takes twenty minutes and costs $18. You can get more information and take the assessment at http://mygreateststrengths.com.

Moving Forward

Whether you are a present or prospective teleworking employee or a manager overseeing one or more teleworkers, just remember that, like any employer–employee relationship, it takes, well, *work* to make it work. It takes trust and honesty, and it takes communication. But we feel that, with a few precautions and continual diligence, the tele-employer–teleworker relationship can be a productive, profitable, and mutually satisfying one.

---

[10] Although you never know.

Could You Work From Home?

The authors of *The Home Office That Works!* have partnered with Peak Focus to offer tools for self-evalution and professional development. Peak Focus is a licensed distributor of the Harrison Assessments, a highly effective and widely respected tool for evaluating potential employees' preferences, motivations and behavioral traits. We've worked with Peak Focus to tailor an Assessment to evaluate those traits that make a good—or bad—teleworker.

What Are Your Greatest Strengths?

Peak Focus has a stripped down assessment called the *Greatest Strengths Report*, an online assessment that will:

- Identify Your Strengths

- Understand Your Challenges

- Really Get to Know Yourself

Knowing your greatest strengths will allow you focus on what you're good at, and let you share the results with prospective employers and on social media like LinkedIn.

KNOW. GROW. SHOW.
your strengths!

It only takes twenty minutes and costs $18. You can get more information and take the assessment at http:// mygreateststrengths.com.

We also offer other evaluations for potential teleworkers. Please visit http://mygreateststrengths.com/product/corporate-telecommuter-analysis/.

Index

Keep Your Home Office Up-to-Date!

The twice monthly *The Home Office That Works!* enewsletter will keep you up to date on the latest news, trends, and resources available to both home office entrepreneurs and telecommuters.

Sign up at http://eepurl.com/btO0dr and get home office-related news, features, story links, data and statistics, hardware and software updates, and important financial, regulatory, and insurance changes delivered right to your inbox. (Sure, your inbox is crowded, but you'll want to make room for this!)

About the Authors

Dr. Joe Webb

Consultant, entrepreneur, and economics commentator Dr. Joe Webb started his career in the industrial imaging industry more than thirty years ago. He found his way into business research, planning, marketing and forecasting executive positions along the way, as well as consulting for firms ranging from large multinationals to small businesses. Dr. Webb started an Internet-based research business in 1995, selling it to a multinational publisher in 2000. Since that time, his consulting, speaking, and research projects have focused on the interaction of business-to-business economics and technology trends. He is a doctoral graduate in industrial and corporate education from New York University, holds an MBA in Management Information Systems from Iona College, with baccalaureate work in managerial sciences and marketing at Manhattan College. He has taught in graduate and undergraduate business programs and resides in North Carolina.

Richard Romano

A professional writer and editor since 1990, he began as an assistant editor in trade book publishing. In the 1990s, he began writing about emerging computer graphics and digital imaging technologies, reviewing some of the earliest digital cameras, scanners, and software. From 1996 to 2001, he was managing editor for *Micro Publishing News* and *Digital Imaging* magazines, writing news stories, features, profiles, and hardware and software reviews. He began collaborating with Dr. Webb in 2000, writing market research reports and officially launching his home office. The collaboration had led to two previous books—*"Does a Plumber Need a Web Site?": Mad Dentists, Harried Haircutters, and Other Edgy Entrepreneurs Offer Promotion Strategies for Small and Mid-Size Businesses* (2012) and *Disrupting the Future: Uncommon Wisdom for Navigating Print's Challenging Marketplace* (2010), the latter of which has since been translated into Japanese and Portuguese. Richard has also authored or co-authored a half dozen or so other books on graphics hardware and software.

Richard has also written, on a freelance basis, everything from quarter-page ads, to e-newsletters, to magazine features, to 200-page market research reports on topics as disparate as laboratory information management systems, the future market for printing presses, and e-book adoption in libraries. He is a frequent speaker on media, communication, and technology trends. He also does freelance writing and graphic design work for local businesses and community organizations in the New York Capital District.

He graduated from Syracuse University's Newhouse School of Public Communications in 1989 with a B.A. in English and Writing for Telecommunications. He also has a certificate in Multimedia Production from New York University (1994) and is nearly finished with a Masters program through the University at Buffalo. He lives in Saratoga Springs, New York.

CPSIA information can be obtained at www.ICGtesting.com
Printed in the USA
LVOW10s1718170516

488656LV00003B/692/P

9 781519 278616